THE ATTACK ON PEARL HARBOR

The Attack on Pearl Harbor

AN ILLUSTRATED HISTORY

Revised Edition

Larry Kimmett

Margaret Regis

Navigator Publishing ❖ Seattle, Washington

Navigator Publishing
P.O. Box 1289
Kingston, WA 98346

Published 1991. Revised Edition 1999.

Printed in the United States of America.

Library of Congress Cataloging-in-Publication Data

Kimmett, Larry.
    The attack on Pearl Harbor : an illustrated history / Larry
  Kimmett, Margaret Regis. — Rev. ed.
        p.   cm.
    Includes bibliographical references and index.
    ISBN 1-879932-04-0 (pbk.)
    1. Pearl Harbor (Hawaii), Attack on, 1941–. 2. Pearl Harbor
  (Hawaii), Attack on, 1941—Pictorial works. I. Regis, Margaret,
  1957–   . II. Title.
D767.92.K55 1999
940.54'26—dc21   99-40261

Cover art by Charles M. Huckeba

Title page illustration: Harbor map captured from Japanese midget submarine

We would like to thank the following individuals and organizations for their generous assistance in the preparation of this book:

Leatrice Arakaki, Hickam Air Force Base
Sharon Culley, National Archives
Roger Dammarell, USMC ret. (USS *New Orleans*)
John Flanagan, *Honolulu Star-Bulletin*
Nick Gaynos, USAAF ret. (Hickam Field)
Carol Gibbens
Donald M. Goldstein, Ph.D.
Charles Haberlein, Jr., Naval Historical Center
Dan Hagedorn, Smithsonian Institution
Paul Hower, USMC ret. (Ewa Marine Corps Air Station)
Charles M. Huckeba
Ken Jones, USN ret. (Kaneohe Naval Air Station)
Bea Kaya, *Honolulu Star-Bulletin*
Richard Earl Laster
Albert Long, USN ret. (Ford Island Naval Air Station)
William Lucius, USMC ret. (Ewa Marine Corps Air Station)
Daniel Martinez, USS Arizona Memorial
Paul McLaughlin, Franklin D. Roosevelt Library
Pearl Harbor Survivors Association
Fred Pernell, National Archives
George J. Sallet, USN ret. (USS *Bagley*)
United States Naval Institute
J. B. Vaessen (USS *Utah*)
Sally Van Natta
Jack C. Weiser, Time-Life
Edward J. White, USAAC ret. (Wheeler Field)
Geoffrey White, Hawaii State Archives

also by Larry Kimmett and Margaret Regis
U.S. Submarines in World War II: An Illustrated History

Contents

War Plan

First Attack Wave

Second Attack Wave

Aftermath

Preface

More than fifty years have passed since the Japanese attack on Pearl Harbor. The two hour battle began a savage forty-four month war between Japan and the United States. Japan's military rulers saw Pearl Harbor as the pivot of a strategic gamble to extricate themselves from their failed war in China. They reasoned Japan might outlast America in a larger war, as it had outlasted Russia in 1905. But the Imperial General Staff miscalculated the nature of total war, the danger of fighting a power ten times stronger, and finally, the profound impact Pearl Harbor would have on the American people.

The Japanese Navy achieved a brilliant technical triumph in the attack and demonstrated the first large scale use of offensive carrier air power in world history. Yet, failure to grasp the critical value of the base itself marred the raid's tactical success. The repair shops, Navy Yard, ammunition dumps, and the exposed oil supply escaped Japanese attention. A few weeks after the assault, Pearl Harbor became and remained the wartime nerve center of the U.S. Navy in the Pacific.

The Americans quickly learned the lessons of naval air power. They absorbed the partial loss of their battleships, and in the epic carrier battles of the Coral Sea, Midway, and Guadalcanal, halted the expansion of the Japanese Empire.

We dedicate this illustrated history of the attack on Pearl Harbor to the Americans who were there.

. . . we here highly resolve that these dead shall not have died in vain . . .

REMEMBER DEC. 7th!

Japan, 1854–1931

In July 1853, four American warships commanded by Commodore Matthew Perry sailed into Tokyo Bay. His orders were to establish a treaty of friendship and commercial relations with the reclusive Japanese. Perry found a feudal society dominated by powerful samurai clans and a military dictator, the shogun.

Despite strong internal opposition to contact with the "barbarians," the shogun bowed to the West's superior military technology and concluded a treaty with the United States in 1854. Several European powers followed the Americans' lead, and extracted their own trade concessions. The shogun's failure to resist these incursions destroyed his legitimacy in the eyes of the Japanese people. In 1868 a group of samurai from western clans overthrew the regime and established a new government led by the one-time figurehead Emperor.

The new Meiji (Enlightened) government realized Japan needed to modernize in all spheres of public life to achieve equality with the West. They began the complete restructuring of the nation's social, political, and economic systems. Meiji authorities abolished feudalism, pensioned off the nobles and their samurai retainers, and reorganized the country into modern administrative prefectures. They also established the Imperial Army, based on conscription, and bought warships from the British for the new Imperial Japanese Navy. Looking to the future, the reformers created a national school program to provide mandatory elementary education. Foundation of the first high schools and universities quickly followed.

To fund these immense development efforts, the Emperor's cabinet began a finance ministry and organized a banking system. State agencies installed a postal service, built new roads, improved ports, and laid the first railways. They also invested in mines, and set up government-owned pilot plants for cotton spinning, silk reeling, and brickmaking. When cash ran short in the 1880s, the Finance Ministry sold off the government's factories to a small group of investors, the *zaibatsu* (financial clique), who thereafter dominated Japan's industrialization.

Determined to maintain the country's conservative traditions while meeting popular demand for political reform, the Meiji government adopted a constitution in 1889. Although this charter established an elected national assembly (Diet), executive power was vested in a cabinet solely responsible to the Emperor. Human rights were guaranteed only "within the limits of the law." At the same time, authorities organized a religious (Shinto) cult in the schools to glorify obedience to the Emperor and his government. Military training became part of the curriculum and reinforced unconditional loyalty to the State.

As Japan's industrial and military strength increased, the country turned overseas for raw materials and new markets. In 1894, Japan fought and defeated China for control of Korea. In the peace settlement, China paid a large indemnity and ceded Formosa (now Taiwan) to the Japanese. Ten years later, Japan went on the offensive again and invaded Russian-controlled southern Manchuria. After numerous engagements, which culminated in the Japanese triumphs at Port Arthur and Tsushima Strait, the Russians yielded the disputed territory.

Japan joined the Allies at the outbreak of World War I in 1914 and declared war on Germany. Imperial forces occupied German possessions in China's Shantung Peninsula and seized the German-controlled Marianas, Caroline, and Marshall islands. Fueled by Allied orders for war materials, Japan's economy grew rapidly during the four year conflict. By the early 1920s, however, industrial overcapacity and increased competition in Asia reduced Japan's material progress to the slowest rate in fifty years. Although self-sufficient in Admiral Perry's day, the country now required continuous economic growth and foreign sources of raw materials and food to support its burgeoning population.

The 1920s ended in the worldwide economic collapse of the Great Depression, which devastated large sectors of Japan's trading economy. The resulting unemployment and misery strengthened the Imperial Army's demand to expand into China to acquire new resources.

Mt. Fuji (left) seen through the periscope of submarine USS *Trigger*, on patrol off the coast of Japan early in World War II. The dormant volcano lies on the Pacific coast of Honshu. At 12,388 ft. it is the highest elevation in Japan. Considered sacred, thousands of pilgrims climb it every year.

13

Causes of War

In September 1931 the Imperial Army, determined to follow its own expansionist course in Asia, invaded Manchuria and set up a puppet state called Manchukuo. When the League of Nations condemned the attack, the Japanese government backed its military and withdrew from the League.

Encouraged by the easy conquest of Manchuria, the Japanese provoked a clash with a Chinese militia unit near Peiping in July 1937. The "China Incident" gave the Imperial General Staff its long-awaited excuse for a full-scale invasion of China. The Japanese occupied large areas along the coast, and the Chinese government retreated into the interior. Eventually the struggle settled into a guerilla war.

Committed to China's independence for a century, the United States responded to the aggression with appropriations for a larger navy and an embargo of strategic materials to Japan.

Early in May 1940, President Roosevelt ordered the U.S. Pacific Fleet moved from California to Pearl Harbor in an unmistakable warning to Japan against further expansion in Asia. Relations between the two countries deteriorated, and in September 1940, Japan joined the Tripartite Pact and aligned itself with Nazi Germany.

War appeared inevitable when Japan invaded French Indochina in July 1941. The U.S. government froze Japanese assets in the United States and cut off all trade, including petroleum. This embargo threatened Japan's vital industries and war machine because the nation imported eighty percent of its oil from the United States. The ruling militarists, led by General Hideki Tojo, decided on a fateful course: seize the tin, rubber, and oil of Southeast Asia.

Japanese Conquests
November 1941

Japanese Controlled

The Emperor Hirohito (top) receives honors during a military review. Although the nominal ruler of the country, the Imperial Army and Navy held the real power in Japan.

By late 1941 (bottom) Japanese aggression had conquered Manchuria, large areas of eastern China, the islands of Formosa, Hainan, and the former French possession of Indochina. Western allies feared the Dutch East Indies would be the next target.

14

A Japanese Naval landing party (left) in China.

Between Dec. 7, 1941 and March 1942 (below) the Japanese planned to conquer Southeast Asia through a series of carefully coordinated surprise attacks—the "Southern Operation." First, they intended to destroy the U.S. Army Air Force on Luzon with air attacks, and then invade the Philippines. At the same time they prepared to land in British Malaya, with the goal of taking Singapore. Japanese forces would also occupy Thailand and Hong Kong in this phase of the operation. Next, the Imperial Army planned an assault on Borneo, the Celebes, and Sumatra. Finally, all forces would combine to seize Java, the richest island in the Dutch East Indies.

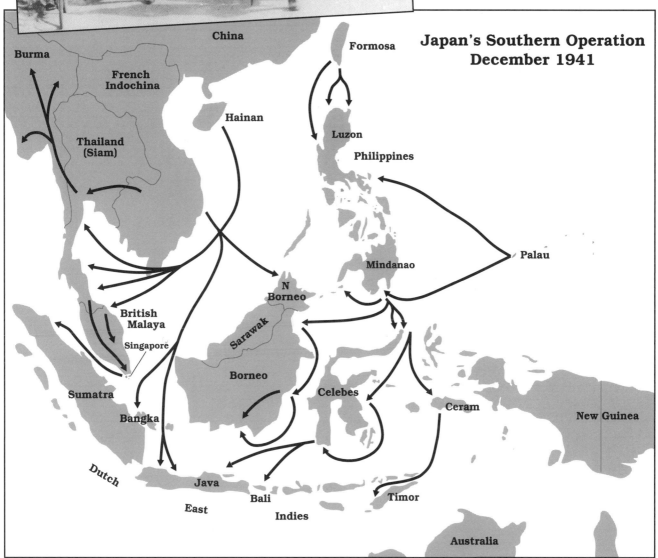

**Japan's Southern Operation
December 1941**

Burma

China

French Indochina

Formosa

Thailand (Siam)

Hainan

Luzon

Philippines

Palau

Mindanao

N Borneo

Sarawak

British Malaya

Singapore

Borneo

Celebes

Ceram

New Guinea

Sumatra

Bangka

Dutch

Java

Bali

Timor

East

Indies

Australia

Pacific Naval Balance—1941

Only the U.S. Pacific Fleet stood in the way of Japan's Southern Operation in late 1941. Although slightly larger than the Japanese Imperial Navy, the U.S. Navy's world-wide responsibilities forced it to divide its ships between the Atlantic and Pacific oceans, giving the Japanese a numerical advantage in the Pacific.

Hitler's conquest of France and Holland the previous summer (1940) left a military vacuum around Southeast Asia's European colonies. With their conquered or embattled mother countries unable to defend them, British Malaya and the Dutch East Indies looked to the United States and its navy to check Japan's territorial ambitions.

The Roosevelt administration quickly took up the challenge. In July 1940 the U.S. Congress passed the Two Ocean Naval Expansion Act which promised to enlarge the U.S. Navy three hundred percent by 1944. Japanese planners knew they could not match the U.S. building program, and the strategic naval balance would inevitably shift to the Americans within three years. If they intended to go to war with the United States, Japan must do so while the Imperial Navy held a numerical superiority in warships.

In the spring of 1941, that superiority increased when heavy convoy demands against the German U-boat menace forced the United States to transfer one-quarter of its Pacific Fleet to the Atlantic. Altogether the naval forces at Pearl Harbor decreased by one aircraft carrier, three battleships, four light cruisers, and seventeen destroyers. The Japanese Navy's Combined Fleet now had ten aircraft carriers to the Americans' three, and twice as many modern cruisers and destroyers.

Japan

16

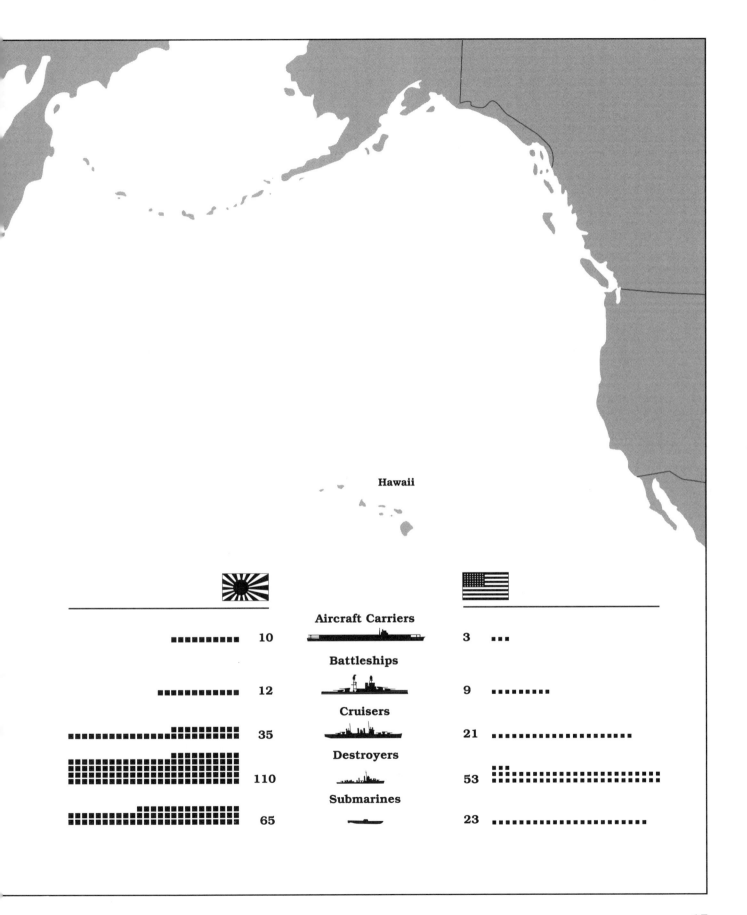

Hawaii

Aircraft Carriers

Japan: 10 United States: 3

Battleships

Japan: 12 United States: 9

Cruisers

Japan: 35 United States: 21

Destroyers

Japan: 110 United States: 53

Submarines

Japan: 65 United States: 23

The Plan

The Japanese attack on the U.S. Pacific Fleet in Hawaii was the first step of the Southern Operation—an ambitious war plan to seize the oil-rich Dutch East Indies, and break the Allied oil embargo.

Admiral Isoroku Yamamoto conceived the Pearl Harbor Attack. The brilliant, fifty-seven-year-old commander of the Combined Fleet believed a decisive aerial strike against the U.S. fleet at Pearl Harbor could shift the strategic balance in Japan's favor and protect the flank of the Southern Operation. Once the Empire constructed a strong defensive perimeter around its conquests, the Americans faced either a peace settlement or a hopeless war of attrition.

Yamamoto began planning the Pearl Harbor raid in January 1941. By late August his staff presented an outline which called for six aircraft carriers to sail from the Kurile Islands through the northern Pacific in late November to a point 200 miles north of Oahu. At dawn on December 7, they would launch 360 planes in two great waves to bomb Pearl Harbor. The objective was to sink all three U.S. aircraft carriers, at least four of the nine battleships, and immobilize the Pacific Fleet for six months to a year.

Meanwhile, the protracted diplomatic negotiations continued in Washington between Japan's special ambassador and Secretary of State Cordell Hull. If the U.S. conceded to demands for a free hand in Asia and ended the oil embargo, the Japanese would cancel the attack. If not, they planned to inform the Americans of the permanent end of negotiations—a virtual declaration of war—just thirty minutes before the first bomb fell on Pearl Harbor.

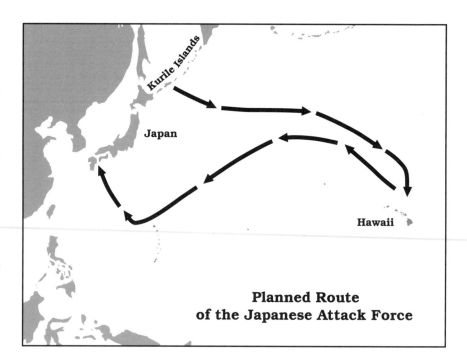

**Planned Route
of the Japanese Attack Force**

The Commanders

Admiral Isoroku Yamamoto wanted to avoid war with the United States. He had studied at Harvard University and served as a naval attaché in Washington, and knew firsthand the war making potential of the Americans. He said: "If I am told to fight regardless of the consequences, I shall run wild for the first six months or a year, but I have utterly no confidence for the second or third year."

Vice Admiral Chuichi Nagumo came to the command of the First Air Fleet after a distinguished career in battleships, cruisers, and destroyers. Although he had little training in naval aviation, Nagumo was a highly capable officer who rose to the challenge. His First Air Fleet won all its battles in the first six months of the war—until Midway—and made him the most successful Japanese admiral of World War II.

The Hawaiian Islands

Niihau

Kauai

Oahu

Molokai

Lanai

Maui

Hawaii

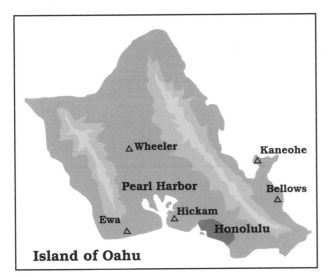

△ Wheeler

Kaneohe △

Pearl Harbor

Bellows △

Ewa △

Hickam △

Honolulu

Island of Oahu

Hawaii became a U.S. territory in 1898, and construction of a naval base at Pearl Harbor

began three years later. Dry dock facilities were finished in 1911, and a submarine base

followed in the early 1920s. When World War II broke out in September 1939, the Army

and Navy began rapid expansion programs to add new facilities to the harbor and the defending airfields. To deter Japanese aggression, the U.S. Pacific Fleet moved permanently from its bases in California to Pearl Harbor in June 1940.

(Below) Aerial view of Pearl Harbor a few weeks before the attack of December 7th.

The Target

The arrival of the U.S. Pacific Fleet from California in June 1940 transformed Oahu and Pearl Harbor. Formerly home to a small cruiser squadron, and site of a submarine base, the sleepy Hawaiian port now found itself host to 3 aircraft carriers, 9 battleships, 12 heavy cruisers, 9 light cruisers, and 53 destroyers.

Pearl Harbor's sudden elevation to a major fleet base created many logistical difficulties. It was a relatively small anchorage for so many vessels. Ships had to be clustered rather than dispersed. Essential materials for fleet training were in short supply, and ships were forced to return to the West Coast for overhaul.

Hawaii lacked adequate housing, and the sudden move separated most of the personnel from their families. Admiral Joseph Richardson, the Pacific Fleet's commander, strenuously objected to President Roosevelt's decision to move the fleet, and, as a consequence, was relieved on February 1, 1941.

Admiral Husband E. Kimmel succeeded Richardson as commander. The new admiral inherited his predecessor's problems, and one more that led to his eventual disgrace: Pearl Harbor's air defenses were almost non-existent.

The U.S. Army, responsible for Oahu's air security, lacked the anti-aircraft guns and fighter defenses to oppose any serious threat. The Army's commander, General Walter Short, believed the main danger to be sabotage from Oahu's large native Japanese population. He ordered the 230 bombers and fighters of his command lined up on their runways to guard against infiltrators. There, the Zeros found them on the morning of December 7th.

The United States Pacific Fleet

Aircraft Carriers: The United States fought and won the war in the Pacific with large carrier task forces. Pearl Harbor and the battles that followed demonstrated the dominance of carrier-borne aircraft and forced the battleship into a supporting role.

USS *Lexington* and USS *Saratoga* Length: 888 feet; Speed: 33 knots; Displacement: 47,700 tons; Aircraft: 80; Guns: eight 8-inch, twelve 5-inch; Crew: 2,100.

USS *Enterprise* Length: 810 feet; Speed: 33 knots; Displacement: 25,500 tons; Aircraft: 80; Guns: eight 5-inch; Crew: 2,000.

Battleships: In December 1941, nine battleships served with the U.S. Pacific Fleet. Eight were at Pearl Harbor, and one, the USS *Colorado* was being overhauled at Puget Sound Navy Yard.

USS *Arizona* and USS *Pennsylvania* Length: 608 feet; Speed: 21 knots; Displacement: 33,000 tons; Guns: twelve 14-inch, twelve 5-inch; Crew: 1,360.

USS *California* and USS *Tennessee* Length: 624 feet; Speed: 21 knots; Displacement: 33,000 tons; Guns: twelve 14-inch, twelve 5-inch; Crew: 1,480.

USS *Maryland* and USS *West Virginia* Length: 624 feet; Speed: 21 knots; Displacement: 32,000 tons; Guns: eight 16-inch, twelve 5-inch; Crew: 1,450.

USS *Oklahoma* and USS *Nevada* Length: 583 feet; Speed: 20 knots; Displacement: 29,000 tons; Guns: ten 14-inch, twelve 5-inch; Crew: 1,300.

Wheeler Field: The main Army Air Force fighter base on Oahu. Combat planes on December 7th: 87 P-40 fighters, 39 obsolete P-36 fighters, and 14 obsolete P-26 fighters. Just north of Wheeler lay Schofield Barracks, a large Army base.

Ewa Marine Air Station: A new base under construction on December 7th, Ewa Marine Air Station was home to 47 planes, including 23 SBD dive-bombers, 11 F4F fighters, and 8 utility planes. All available aircraft were kept on two-hour alert.

Kaneohe Naval Air Station: New PBY "Catalina" seaplane patrol base. Home of patrol squadrons VP 11, VP 12, and VP 14 (36 PBYs). These planes represented a significant part of Oahu's long range reconnaissance capability.

Bellows Field: U.S. Army Air Force auxiliary training base. Home for a small number of observation planes. Fighter squadrons used Bellows during rotating gunnery training periods. Twelve P-40 fighters were there on December 7th.

Targets on Oahu

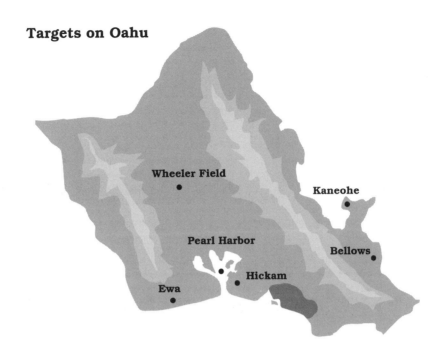

Wheeler Field

Kaneohe

Pearl Harbor

Bellows

Ewa

Hickam

Pearl Harbor: Home port of the U.S. Pacific Fleet after June 1940. Main fleet units: 3 aircraft carriers, 9 battleships, 12 heavy cruisers, 9 light cruisers, 53 destroyers, and 23 submarines. Organized into three major task forces, one of which was always at sea.

Hickam Air Field: Main U.S. Army Air Force bomber base on Oahu. Combat planes on December 7th: 12 B-17s (heavy bombers), 32 obsolete B-18s (medium bombers), and 12 A-20s (light bombers). Twelve B-17s from California arrived during the attack.

Cruisers: Japan began World War II with 35 cruisers to the U.S. Pacific Fleet's 21. During the war the U.S. built 46 and Japan only 5.

USS *New Orleans* and USS *San Francisco* Length: 588 feet; Speed: 33 knots; Displacement: 9,950 tons; Guns: nine 8-inch, eight 5-inch AA; Crew: 550.

USS *St. Louis* and USS *Helena* Length: 608 feet; Speed: 33 knots; Displacement:10,000 tons; Guns: fifteen 6-inch, eight 5-inch; Crew: 888.

USS *Raleigh* and USS *Detroit* Length: 556 feet; Speed: 35 knots; Displacement: 7,050 tons; Guns: ten 6-inch; four 3-inch AA; Crew: 460.

Destroyers: The U.S. Pacific Fleet entered World War II with 53 destroyers, but some of these were old four-funnel ships built in World War I.

Porter class destroyer Length: 381 feet; Speed: 37 knots; Displacement: 1,835 tons; Guns: eight 5-inch, eight 1.1-inch; Crew: 194.

Mahan class destroyer Length: 341 feet; Speed: 36 knots; Displacement: 1,488 tons; Guns: five 5-inch; four 50 caliber machine guns; Crew: 158.

Submarines: The U.S. Navy entered World War II with 113 submarines, 23 serving with the Pacific Fleet. During the war 228 more were built.

Tambor class submarine Length: 310 feet; Speed:17 knots/9 knots; Displacement: 1,450 tons; Guns: one 3-inch, 10 torpedo tubes; Crew: 55.

The Weapon—*Kido Butai*

The Japanese invented a new naval weapon to attack the U.S. Fleet at Pearl Harbor: the carrier task force. For the first time in world history, six aircraft carriers combined into a single unit to create an aerial armada of over 350 planes.

Designated the First Air Fleet, the Pearl Harbor strike force consisted of the carriers, *Akagi, Kaga, Soryu, Hiryu, Shokaku,* and *Zuikaku.* A screen of 2 fast battleships, 2 heavy cruisers, 1 light cruiser, 9 destroyers, and 3 picket submarines escorted the carriers. Eight tankers accompanied the group to refuel the task force vessels. Altogether, 31 Japanese warships sailed in mid-November 1941 for their secret rendezvous in the Kurile Islands to prepare for the Hawaii attack.

The Imperial Navy assembled other special arms for the raid. Torpedoes were the most effective weapon against ships, but ordinary types hit bottom if dropped in shallow depths. Through intensive work, technicians devised torpedoes to run true in Pearl Harbor's forty foot waters.

The Navy's ordnance section converted 16-inch shells into aerial bombs to penetrate the five-inch thick steel decks of American battleships. Finally, the strike force carried a full complement of Japan's new Zeros—their best fighters—to guarantee air superiority.

The Japanese knew seaborne air power had been used once before to attack ships in harbor. The previous year, 1940, twenty-one torpedo planes from the British carrier *Illustrious* seriously damaged three Italian battleships in a night attack on the Mediterranean port of Taranto. The First Air Fleet's assault was fifteen times larger than the Taranto raid.

Pearl Harbor Attack Force

Aircraft Carriers. By 1941 the Japanese had six fleet carriers and four auxiliary carriers in commission. The U.S. Navy, in contrast, had seven fleet carriers in operation—only three of them stationed in the Pacific.

Akagi ("Red Castle") Length: 856 feet; Speed: 31 knots; Aircraft: 63; Guns: ten 8-inch, twelve 4.7-inch; Crew: 1,600.

Kaga ("Increased Joy") Length: 783 feet; Speed: 28 knots; Aircraft: 63; Guns: ten 8-inch, twelve 4.7-inch; Crew: 1,700.

Soryu ("Green Dragon") Length: 746 feet; Speed: 34 knots; Aircraft: 54; Guns: twelve 5-inch, twenty-eight 1-inch; Crew: 1,100.

Hiryu ("Flying Dragon") Length: 746 feet; Speed: 34 knots; Aircraft: 54; Guns: twelve 5-inch, twenty-eight 1-inch; Crew: 1,100.

Shokaku ("Soaring Crane") Length: 845 feet; Speed: 34 knots; Aircraft: 72; Guns: sixteen 5-inch, twenty-eight 1-inch; Crew: 1,700.

Zuikaku ("Happy Crane") Length: 845 feet; Speed: 34 knots; Aircraft: 72; Guns: sixteen 5-inch, twenty-eight 1-inch; Crew: 1,700.

The aircraft carrier *Kaga* (left) on the way to Pearl Harbor. The Japanese went to great lengths to conceal the departure of the First Air Fleet. Naval bases in mainland Japan gave extra shore leave to mask the absence of so many sailors. The First Air Fleet kept radio silence, while shore stations maintained a phony ship-to-shore radio traffic to suggest that Japan's carriers were in home port. In addition, ship radio call signs were changed on December 1st to confuse U.S. Naval monitoring stations around the Pacific.

Zeros (below) warm up on the deck of a First Air Fleet carrier. *Akagi* and *Kaga* each carried 63 aircraft: 18 Val dive-bombers, 18 Zero fighters, and 27 Kate high-level bombers. The smaller *Soryu* and *Hiryu* fielded 54 planes—18 of each kind. The newly commissioned *Shokaku* and *Zuikaku* carried 72 aircraft: 18 Zero fighters, 27 Val dive-bombers, and 27 Kate bombers.

Fuchida's Chart

Lt. Comdr. Fuchida's operational plan assigned specific targets to each group of his aircraft. In the first attack wave, the Nakajima B5N2 three-man bomber (Allied code name "Kate") carried out the torpedo and high-level bombing efforts. Fuchida allotted forty Kates to the critical torpedo attack, and forty-nine more to drop their large armor-piercing bomb on the battleships moored inboard beyond the range of the torpedo planes.

To ensure the Kates reached the warships of the Pacific Fleet unhindered by U.S. fighter planes, twenty-five Aichi D3A1 dive-bombers (Allied code name "Val") targeted the main American fighter base at Wheeler Field. Nine more Vals were to hit the Navy fighter and patrol plane base at Ford Island, while the remaining seventeen struck the bomber base at nearby Hickam Field.

The Japanese deployed forty-three Mitsubishi A6M2 fighters (Allied code name "Zero") in the first attack wave to shoot down any U.S. fighters that managed to escape the dive-bombers. They also planned to use the Zeros' formidable 20 mm cannons and 7.7 mm machine guns offensively to strafe American aircraft caught on the ground.

In the second assault wave, Fuchida committed fifty-four Kates to the high-level bombing of the airfields. He allocated twenty-seven Kate bombers, each armed with two 550 pound bombs, to Hickam Field, nine to Ford Island, and eighteen to Kaneohe Naval Air Station. Eighty Vals, the largest single contingent, were to dive-bomb undamaged ships and the Pearl Harbor Navy Yard. Thirty-six Zeros escorted the second wave to protect the bombers and continue strafing attacks on the air bases.

Japanese Carrier Aircraft

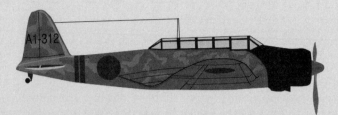

Nakajima B5N2 (Kate): Built by the Nakajima Company for the Imperial Navy in the late 1930s, the B5N2 was the finest torpedo bomber in the world in 1941. The plane could carry its crew of three at 230 mph with a load of 1,764 lbs., either one torpedo or several bombs. One hundred and forty-three Kates were used in the two attack waves at Pearl Harbor. Their successes included the sinking of the battleships *West Virginia*, *Oklahoma*, and *California* by torpedo attack, and the destruction of the battleship *Arizona* by high-level bombing.

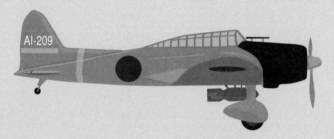

Aichi D3A1 (Val): This dive-bomber proved to be one of the most versatile aircraft of the early Pacific War. The Val could carry a 550 lb. bomb under the fuselage and one 132 lb. bomb under each wing. Its fixed undercarriage added stability and made it so maneuverable it could be used as a fighter plane. The two man crew had three machine guns for strafing or aerial combat. During the attack, Vals sank the destroyers *Cassin*, *Downes*, and *Shaw*, and damaged the battleship *Nevada*. The Americans shot down fifteen Vals.

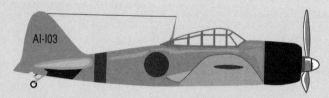

Mitsubishi A6M2 (Zero): This fighter shocked the Allies in the opening months of the Pacific War. With a top speed of 330 mph, it was faster and more agile than any Allied fighter until the middle of 1943. Heavily armed with two 20 mm cannon and two 7.7 mm machine guns, it allowed the Imperial Navy to achieve air superiority in the first six months of the war. Zero fighters destroyed aircraft at Hickam, Wheeler, Kaneohe, and Ewa airfields. Seventy-nine Zeros flew in the attack, and nine were shot down.

Air Attack Force

Thirty-nine-year-old Lt. Commander Mitsuo Fuchida led the air groups of the First Air Fleet in their attack on Pearl Harbor. A veteran airman with over 3,000 hours of flying time, and an expert in high-level bombing, Fuchida served as commander of the First Air Fleet from September 1941 to June 1942 when he was wounded at the battle of Midway. After the war he became a Protestant minister in the United States. He later wrote: "That morning . . . I lifted the curtain of warfare by dispatching that cursed order. . . ."

	Type of Plane	Carrier	Planes Launched*	Armament	Target
First Wave Mitsuo Fuchida commanding 7:55 AM	Kate High-Level Bombers	Akagi Kaga Soryu Hiryu	15 14 10 10 } 49	One 1,750 lb. armor piercing bomb	Battleships
	Kate Torpedo Bombers	Akagi Kaga Soryu Hiryu	12 12 8 8 } 40	One 1,750 lb. air torpedo	Battleships Cruisers
	Val Dive-Bombers	Shokaku Zuikaku	26 25 } 51	One 550 lb. bomb	Ford Island, Hickam & Wheeler Air Bases
	Zero Fighters	Akagi Kaga Soryu Hiryu Shokaku Zuikaku	9 9 8 6 5 6 } 43	Two 20 mm machine guns Two 7.7 mm machine guns	Ford Island Air Base Hickam Air Base Wheeler Air Base Ewa Air Base Kaneohe Air Base
Second Wave Shigekazu Shimazaki commanding 8:54 AM	Kate High-Level Bombers	Zuikaku Shokaku	27 27 } 54	550 lb. bombs or 125 lb. bombs	Hickam, Ford Island & Kaneohe Air Bases
	Val Dive-Bombers	Soryu Hiryu Akagi Kaga	17 17 18 26 } 78	One 550 lb. bomb	Cruisers Battleships Destroyers
	Zero Fighters	Akagi Kaga Soryu Hiryu	9 9 9 8 } 35	Two 20 mm machine guns Two 7.7 mm machine guns	Ford Island Air Base Hickam Air Base Wheeler Air Base Kaneohe Air Base

* Ten planes aborted due to mechanical difficulties.

Special Attack Force

Although the "Hawaii Operation" (code name for the Pearl Harbor raid) relied on carrier aircraft to destroy the U.S. Pacific Fleet, the Japanese had never tried a large scale aerial attack on a defended harbor. Doubts persisted about the outcome. The Naval General Staff decided to add a submarine force to guarantee success.

At the start of the Pacific War in December 1941, the Japanese Navy had sixty-three operational submarines. Twenty-seven modern boats, part of Japan's Sixth Fleet, took part in the Pearl Harbor raid. Four subs patrolled in a picket line north of Oahu, while the remaining submarines deployed at positions around the Hawaiian Islands. They had four missions: first, to conduct reconnaissance in the Oahu area; second, to torpedo U.S. warships escaping from Pearl Harbor; and third, to intercept any naval counterattack against Nagumo's six carriers.

Finally, five submarines each carried a two-man midget sub (the Special Attack Force) to a point just outside Pearl Harbor. Once released in the early morning hours of December 7th, the battery-powered midgets planned to enter the harbor submerged, rest on the bottom until the attack began, then launch their torpedoes in the confusion, and escape. The mother subs would remain in the area to pick them up that night.

Late on December 6th, the five large submarines approached Oahu on the surface. Crews of the midget subs could see the lights of Waikiki Beach when they climbed into their boats about midnight. A few minutes later, the larger ships submerged and picked up speed to give the midgets a start. At the signal, four steel clamps released, and the small subs floated free.

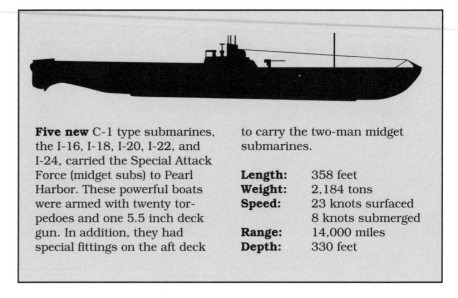

Five new C-1 type submarines, the I-16, I-18, I-20, I-22, and I-24, carried the Special Attack Force (midget subs) to Pearl Harbor. These powerful boats were armed with twenty torpedoes and one 5.5 inch deck gun. In addition, they had special fittings on the aft deck to carry the two-man midget submarines.

Length:	358 feet
Weight:	2,184 tons
Speed:	23 knots surfaced
	8 knots submerged
Range:	14,000 miles
Depth:	330 feet

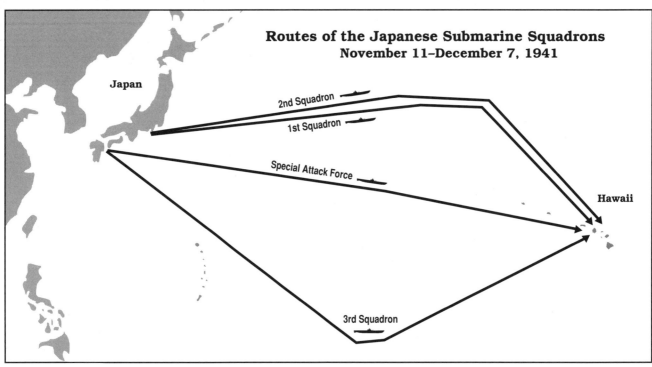

Routes of the Japanese Submarine Squadrons
November 11–December 7, 1941

Japan

2nd Squadron

1st Squadron

Special Attack Force

Hawaii

3rd Squadron

To ensure destruction of the U.S. Pacific Fleet, Japan surrounded Oahu with a submarine armada. Although the subs sank several merchant ships after the attack on December 7th, and made two unsuccessful attempts to torpedo the aircraft carrier *Enterprise*, no U.S. warships fell victim to the submarine pack. On December 10, aircraft from the USS *Enterprise* caught the *I-70* on the surface 200 miles from Oahu and sank it with all hands.

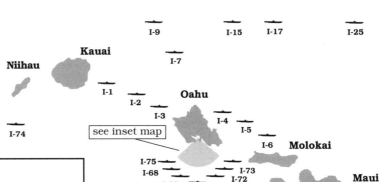

Japanese Submarine Positions Around Hawaii
December 7, 1941

I-9 I-15 I-17 I-25

I-7

Niihau   Kauai

I-1

I-2   Oahu

I-3   I-4

I-5

see inset map

I-6   Molokai

I-74

I-75   I-73   Maui

I-68   I-72

I-69   I-71

I-70   Lanai

Hawaii

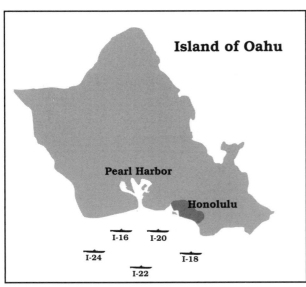

Island of Oahu

Pearl Harbor

Honolulu

I-16   I-20

I-24   I-18

I-22

The Japanese Navy developed midget submarines in the 1930s. They were to be ferried to their combat areas by specially fitted attack submarines. Each midget sub was 78.5 feet long, weighed 46 tons, carried two crewmen, and was armed with two torpedoes.

A battery-driven electric motor gave it a speed of 23 knots on the surface and 19 knots underwater. Its range was 80 miles surfaced and 18 miles submerged. All five midget subs were lost in the attack on Pearl Harbor.

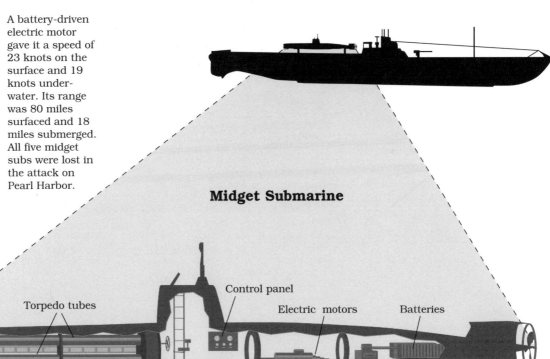

Midget Submarine

Control panel

Electric motors

Batteries

Torpedo tubes

27

On the Way

In late November 1941, the First Air Fleet, designated *Kido Butai* (Carrier Striking Force), assembled in Hitokappu Bay, a remote harbor in the cold, foggy Kurile Islands. On November 25th, Vice Admiral Nagumo received his orders from Tokyo. The strike force was to sail November 26th, refuel at sea, and on the morning of December 7th, launch an attack on Pearl Harbor.

The next day at dawn, thirty-one ships raised anchor and departed on their twelve-day, 4,000 mile voyage. Keeping well outside normal sea lanes, the fleet maintained strict radio silence. Stormy winter weather hampered sailing in formation and caused the loss of one sailor, swept overboard during refueling. Despite the rough seas, the warships kept one-quarter of their crews on deck at battle stations throughout the long journey.

On December 2nd, Admiral Yamamoto sent Vice Admiral Nagumo the prearranged code, ordering the attack: "Climb Mount Niitaka." The next day, after refueling the fleet, the accompanying tankers left to await its return at a rendevous point for the voyage back to Japan. The task force continued at 13 knots toward the launch position. All across the Pacific Japanese forces prepared for simultaneous attack on their targets. In Honolulu, the Japanese Consulate staff maintained covert surveillance of Pearl Harbor and kept Tokyo and Nagumo's fleet informed of last minute U.S. warship dispositions.

At 9 p.m. on December 6th Nagumo called all hands on deck and read Admiral Yamamoto's battle order: "The rise or fall of the Empire depends on this battle. Everyone will do his duty to the utmost." The First Air Fleet then turned south and raced forward at 26 knots.

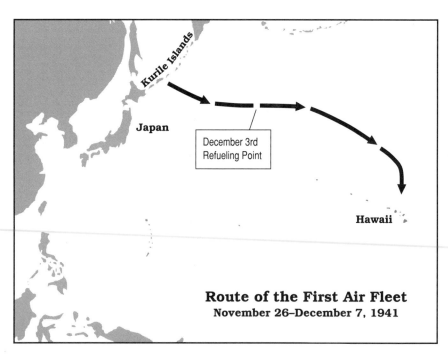

Route of the First Air Fleet
November 26–December 7, 1941

December 3rd Refueling Point

Kurile Islands

Japan

Hawaii

After careful study (top) Japanese naval planners chose a northern approach to Hawaii for the First Air Fleet. Although this route traversed rough seas, and made ship refueling a dangerous task, it had two advantages for the Japanese: American patrols were weakest in the area north of Oahu, and the poor December weather would hide the fleet's position.

While the First Air Fleet (above) sailed eastward at 13 knots to conserve fuel, dozens of lookouts scanned the sea for enemy planes, ships, or submarines. Flight crews tuned up their aircraft to peak mechanical condition. Pilots studied scale models of Oahu and Pearl Harbor until they were completely familiar with their individual attack routes and targets.

Formation of the Japanese Fleet

On the night of December 6th, Nagumo's fleet rushed toward Oahu to reach the launch point by dawn. The light cruiser *Abukuma* and four destroyers headed the column. Battleships *Hiei* and *Kirishima*, flanked by heavy cruisers *Tone* and *Chikuma*, followed. Three miles astern, the six aircraft carriers surged forward, while destroyers and submarines came up as the rear guard. Aboard the carriers many pilots awoke early to prepare for the upcoming attack. Some finished farewell letters home while others enjoyed a special breakfast. After the meal the pilots gathered in each carrier's ready room for a final briefing. Aboard *Akagi* Commander Fuchida went over the attack plan one last time. They were ready.

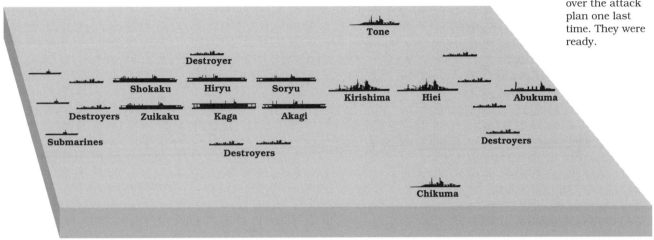

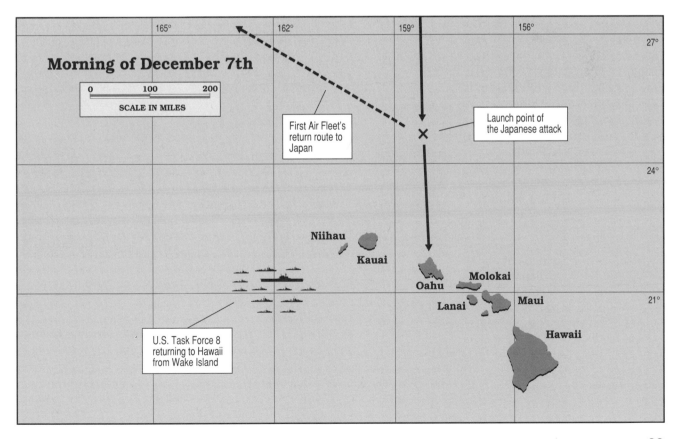

The Launch

Just before dawn on December 7th, the Japanese task force reached its launch point 230 miles north of Oahu. While the warships crashed through rough seas, dozens of planes warmed their engines on each carrier's flight deck. Sentimental music from radio station KGMB in Honolulu reassured senior officers that the fleet remained undetected. About 5:30 a.m. the First Air Fleet sent out two Zero-type planes in advance of the attack to scout Pearl Harbor and the area around Oahu.

Forty-five minutes later, at 6:15 a.m., the six carriers swung into the wind to allow the aircraft to take off. Crews lined the flight decks, shouting "*Banzai,*" and the signals officer raised his lamp. Forty-three Zero fighters, the lightest planes, launched first.

Forty-nine high-level bombers followed, each weighed down by its one-ton bomb. Fifty-one dive-bombers took off next, and finally, 40 torpedo planes roared down the pitching decks. By 6:30, 183 planes of the first wave had been launched. Only two fighters failed to get into the air—one crashed and the other developed engine trouble.

With the first attack on its way, the carriers' flight hands worked to ready the planes of the next wave. One by one, the elevators brought the aircraft up to the flight decks, where crews spotted them for take-off.

At 7:15 a.m. the first fighter gunned its engine and headed down *Akagi's* deck. The launch followed the original order: 35 Zero fighters, 54 Kate high-level bombers, and 78 Val dive-bombers. By 7:30, the second group of 167 aircraft joined formation and began the flight to Pearl Harbor. A total of 350 Japanese planes were on the way to attack the U.S. Pacific Fleet.

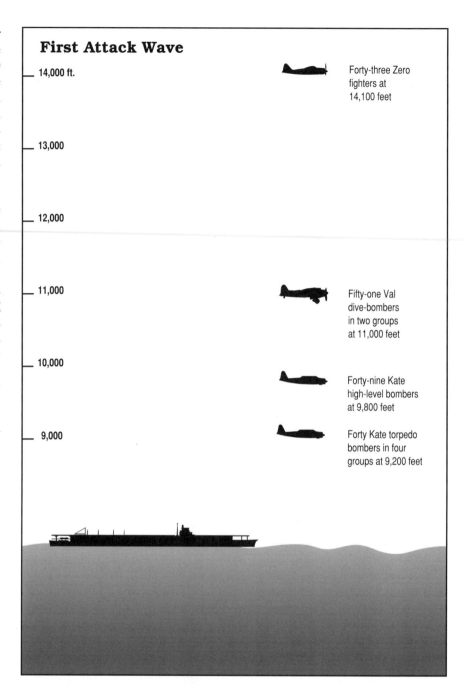

First Attack Wave

- 14,000 ft.
- 13,000
- 12,000
- 11,000
- 10,000
- 9,000

Forty-three Zero fighters at 14,100 feet

Fifty-one Val dive-bombers in two groups at 11,000 feet

Forty-nine Kate high-level bombers at 9,800 feet

Forty Kate torpedo bombers in four groups at 9,200 feet

On December 7th in the half light of dawn, individual planes joined their attack groups, circling above the ships. Marked by an orange light, Commander Fuchida's plane led the growing body of aircraft. After fifteen minutes, the 183 plane strike force attained formation. Fuchida flew across flagship *Akagi's* bow, the signal to head south for Oahu.

For the ninety minute flight to Pearl Harbor the attack wave (above) divided into four large groups: Kate torpedo bombers formed a right flank at 9,200 feet, Kate high-level bombers flew in the center at 9,800 feet, Val dive-bombers held the left at 11,000 feet, and Zero fighters protected the entire force at 14,100 feet.

Crewmen (top right) shout *"Banzai"* (lit. "10,000 years") as another Kate takes off. Aboard *Akagi* Admiral Nagumo hoisted the famous "Z" flag, the same ensign used by Admiral Togo in Japan's great naval victory over Russia in 1905.

30

A torpedo bomber (left) leaves the deck of a Japanese carrier. During the Pearl Harbor attack, the First Air Fleet's planes carried forty special model II Mitsubishi torpedoes—the best in the world in 1941. Although the Americans shot down five Kates from the carrier *Kaga*, twenty-one torpedo bombers hit their targets. Torpedoes caused most of the serious ship damage to the U.S. fleet, including the sinking of the battleships *West Virginia*, *Oklahoma*, and *California*.

Early Warnings

In the early morning hours of December 7th, two warnings of the impending attack occurred. At 6:40 a.m. *Antares*, a supply ship, approached Pearl Harbor and spotted a small submarine's conning tower in the forbidden defensive zone. *Antares'* captain notified the patrolling destroyer *Ward*, which in turn, came up, spotted the midget sub, and opened fire with its deck guns. The second round hit the sub. *Ward* then crossed the spot and and sank the sub with a pattern of depth charges. The destroyer's captain promptly reported the fight to the Naval District's watch officer. The chain of command was still debating its significance when the first bombs fell.

The second warning occurred at 7:02 a.m., nearly half an hour after the *Ward* fired the first shot of America's Pacific War. Two Army radar operators at the Opana station above Kahuku Point on Oahu's north shore picked up a large formation of planes on their radar screen. After checking and rechecking the equipment, they notified the Fort Shafter information center. A pursuit officer believed the planes to be a group of B-17s flying in from California, and took no action.

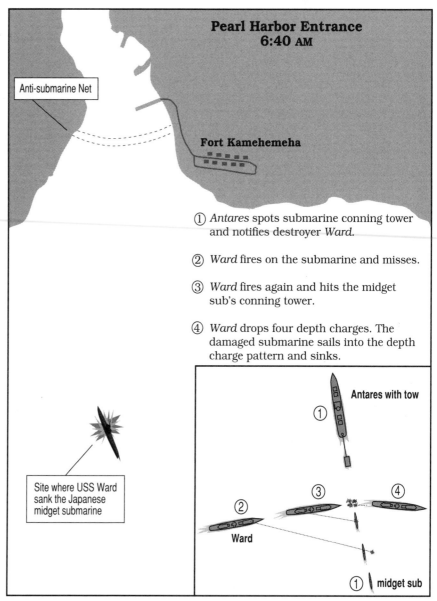

**Pearl Harbor Entrance
6:40 AM**

Anti-submarine Net

Fort Kamehemeha

① *Antares* spots submarine conning tower and notifies destroyer *Ward*.

② *Ward* fires on the submarine and misses.

③ *Ward* fires again and hits the midget sub's conning tower.

④ *Ward* drops four depth charges. The damaged submarine sails into the depth charge pattern and sinks.

Antares with tow

Site where USS Ward sank the Japanese midget submarine

Ward

① **midget sub**

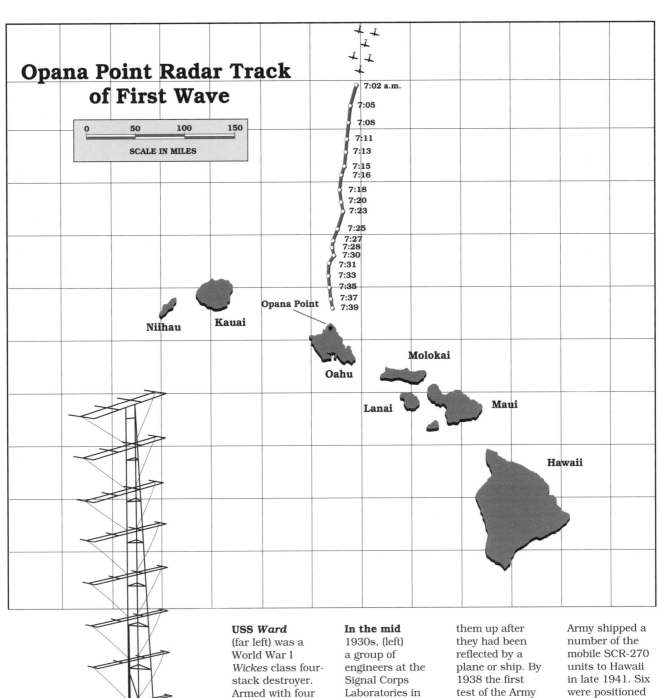

Opana Point Radar Track of First Wave

SCALE IN MILES
0   50   100   150

7:02 a.m.
7:05
7:08
7:11
7:13
7:15
7:16
7:18
7:20
7:23
7:25
7:27
7:28
7:30
7:31
7:33
7:35
7:37
7:39

Niihau   Kauai   Opana Point

Oahu

Molokai

Lanai   Maui

Hawaii

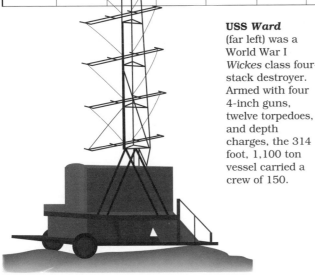

USS *Ward* (far left) was a World War I *Wickes* class four-stack destroyer. Armed with four 4-inch guns, twelve torpedoes, and depth charges, the 314 foot, 1,100 ton vessel carried a crew of 150.

In the mid 1930s, (left) a group of engineers at the Signal Corps Laboratories in Fort Monmouth, New Jersey began development work on radar (**Ra**dio **D**etecting **A**nd **R**anging). This new military technology used a transmitter to send out high-frequency radio waves, and a receiver to pick them up after they had been reflected by a plane or ship. By 1938 the first test of the Army SCR-270 mobile early warning radar unit was completed. Westinghouse Corp. received a production contract in August 1940. They manufactured over one hundred sets before December 7, 1941. The Army shipped a number of the mobile SCR-270 units to Hawaii in late 1941. Six were positioned around the coast of Oahu on December 7th, including the northernmost one at Opana Point. Lacking spare transmitters, the radar units limited their operations to a few hours in the early morning.

Last Moment of Peace

Sunday December 7th, 7:45 a.m. Honolulu time, Secretary of State Cordell Hull prepared to meet Japanese Ambassador Nomura and special envoy Kurusu in Washington, D.C. He knew from Naval Intelligence that the diplomat had received secret instructions to reject America's latest peace proposal, and to break off negotiations.

At Pearl Harbor, Admiral Kimmel maintained a partial alert. Ships kept one-quarter of their anti-aircraft batteries ready, and destroyers were under orders to depth bomb any submerged contact in the defensive zone. Yet the fleet did not expect attack. There were not enough long-range planes for patrols, and the early warning radar system operated only for training. All eyes turned to the Far East where war might break out at any hour, but now that war had come to Hawaii.

U.S. sailors (right) on liberty at Waikiki Beach before the attack. A first class seaman earned $54.00 a month in 1941.

Pearl Harbor (below) in October 1941. On Sunday morning December 7th the sun rose over Oahu at 6:26 a.m. The day was clear and warm with a light breeze from the northeast. Church bells from Honolulu rang softly over Pearl Harbor while the sailors ate breakfast, read, wrote letters, or talked. At 8 a.m. ships' details would hoist the Stars and Stripes.

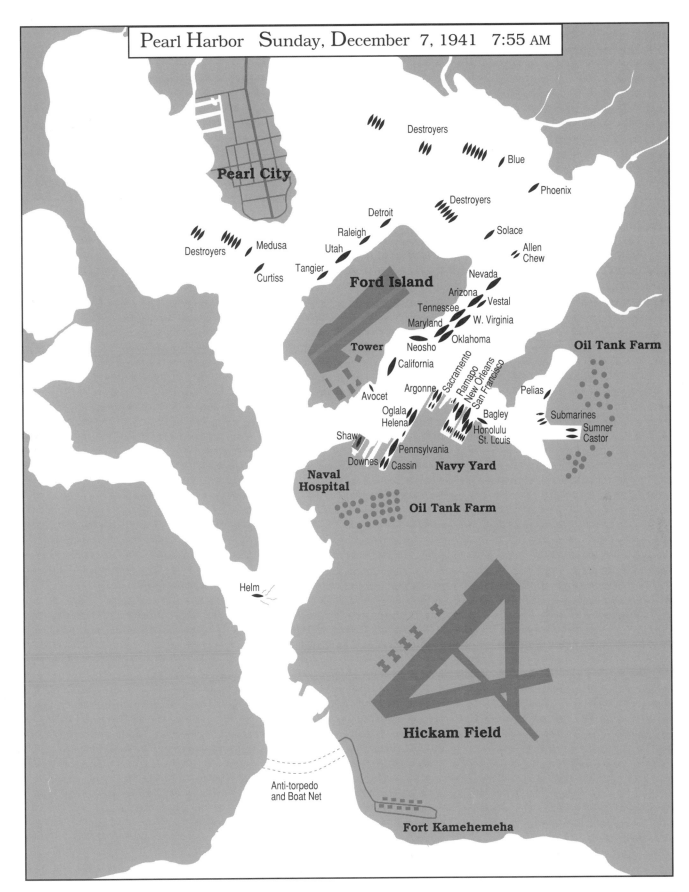

Pearl Harbor Sunday, December 7, 1941 7:55 AM

Destroyers

Blue

Phoenix

Pearl City

Destroyers

Detroit

Solace

Destroyers

Raleigh

Allen
Chew

Utah

Nevada

Destroyers

Medusa

Tangier

Ford Island

Arizona

Vestal

Curtiss

Tennessee

W. Virginia

Maryland

Oklahoma

Tower

Neosho

Oil Tank Farm

California

Sacramento

Argonne

Ramapo

Pelias

Avocet

New Orleans

San Francisco

Oglala

Bagley

Submarines

Helena

Honolulu

Sumner

St. Louis

Castor

Shaw

Pennsylvania

Downes

Cassin

Navy Yard

Naval
Hospital

Oil Tank Farm

Helm

Hickam Field

Anti-torpedo
and Boat Net

Fort Kamehemeha

Tora, Tora, Tora

At 7:40 a.m. Lt. Comdr. Fuchida, leading the first group of 183 planes, spotted the north shore of Oahu. He fired a single rocket flare to signal "surprise," and to tell the slower torpedo planes to go in first. His dive-bombers misread the signal and began their attack.

Fuchida's anger over this tactical mistake quickly dissipated when he looked through his binoculars and saw Battleship Row. Seven battleships moored on the east side of Ford Island. The light cruisers *Raleigh* and *Detroit,* the target ship *Utah,* and the seaplane tender *Tangier* lay at anchor on the west side of the island. Three light and two heavy cruisers berthed at the Navy Yard docks, while twenty-eight destroyers in small groups swung at anchor around Ford Island and the adjacent lochs. Over twenty fleet service vessels were scattered among the warships.

Fuchida saw the battleship *Pennsylvania* sitting in Dry Dock 1 with the destroyers *Cassin* and *Downes.* Another destroyer, the *Shaw,* awaited repairs in Dry Dock 2. Three submarines tied up at the sub base, distinguished by its 119 foot training tower.

Altogether ninety-six ships sat in Pearl Harbor, but the best targets, the three U.S. aircraft carriers were gone. The carrier *Lexington,* with escort, was on its way to Midway to deliver a squadron of Marine bombers. The carrier *Saratoga,* sister ship to the *Lexington,* was in San Diego for repairs and general overhaul. Carrier *Enterprise,* with an escort of three cruisers and nine destroyers, was returning from a supply mission to Wake Island. The *Enterprise* group was due in Pearl Harbor at 6 a.m., but a storm delayed its return, and the task force was now 200 miles west of Oahu.

At 7:52 a.m. Lt. Comdr. Fuchida ordered his radioman to send a signal to the carrier *Akagi:* "*Tora, Tora, Tora*" (Tiger, Tiger, Tiger), the code for complete strategic surprise.

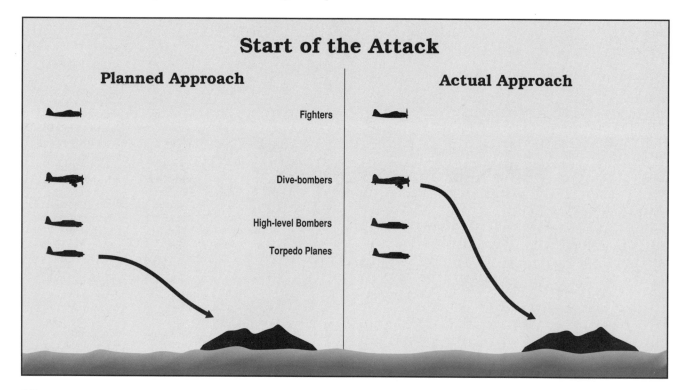

First Attack Wave
7:55 AM

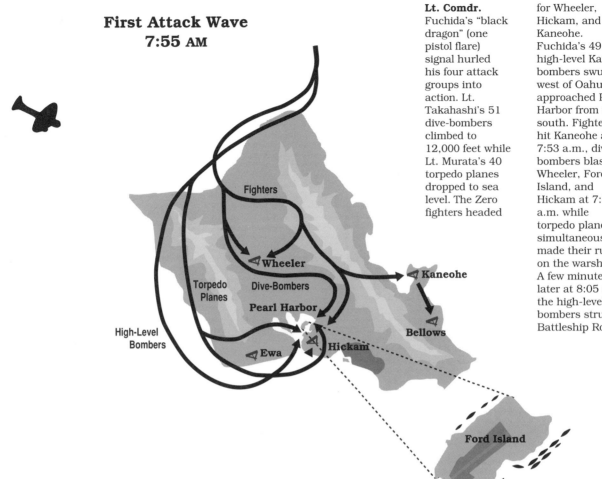

Fighters

Wheeler

Kaneohe

Torpedo Planes

Dive-Bombers

Pearl Harbor

High-Level Bombers

Bellows

Ewa

Hickam

Ford Island

Lt. Comdr. Fuchida's "black dragon" (one pistol flare) signal hurled his four attack groups into action. Lt. Takahashi's 51 dive-bombers climbed to 12,000 feet while Lt. Murata's 40 torpedo planes dropped to sea level. The Zero fighters headed for Wheeler, Hickam, and Kaneohe. Fuchida's 49 high-level Kate bombers swung west of Oahu and approached Pearl Harbor from the south. Fighters hit Kaneohe at 7:53 a.m., dive-bombers blasted Wheeler, Ford Island, and Hickam at 7:55 a.m. while torpedo planes simultaneously made their runs on the warships. A few minutes later at 8:05 a.m. the high-level bombers struck Battleship Row.

The seaplane hangar (left) at the southern end of Ford Island Naval Air Station. Nine Val dive-bombers opened the attack on Pearl Harbor with a strike against Patrol Squadrons 22 and 23, based at this facility. Within a few minutes most of the two squadrons' 26 planes were destroyed. In the lull between the attacks, at 8:30 a.m., air station crewmen tried to repair the less damaged planes. Even though the hangars were burning, an old supply officer refused to issue spare parts without signed orders. When the commander of Patrol Wing Two, Rear Admiral Patrick Bellinger, heard about the delay, he led a group of Marines to the supply depot and ordered them to take whatever they needed.

Torpedo Attack

Forty Kate torpedo bombers began their descent to Pearl Harbor when Fuchida signaled the attack. Dropping down from 9,200 feet, they split into two groups; sixteen torpedo planes approached from the northwest side of Ford Island while twenty-four planes swung over Hickam Field and attacked from the southeast.

The group of sixteen torpedo planes found a pair of light cruisers, *Raleigh* and *Detroit,* and an old target battleship, *Utah,* where the aircraft carriers *Lexington* and *Enterprise* normally moored. Despite orders to ignore these lighter warships, the pilots launched six torpedoes before they realized better targets awaited them on the other side of Ford Island.

Three torpedoes slammed into the port side of the USS *Utah* which immediately began to capsize. The commander ordered all hands to abandon ship. Japanese planes strafed the men as they went over the starboard side into the oily water. Meanwhile, another torpedo exploded below the bridge of USS *Raleigh,* flooding the forward engine room.

By now the second attack group of twenty-four torpedo planes lined up and roared down the long East Loch which led like a bowling alley to Battleship Row. A marine standing on the stern of the USS *New Orleans* exchanged a glance with the pilot of a torpedo plane as he flew by at fifty feet.

Attacking in groups of three, the pilots remembered their orders to concentrate on a few ships to ensure complete destruction. The USS *West Virginia* and USS *Oklahoma* had the misfortune to be centered in front of the planes when they streaked toward Battleship Row at 100 knots.

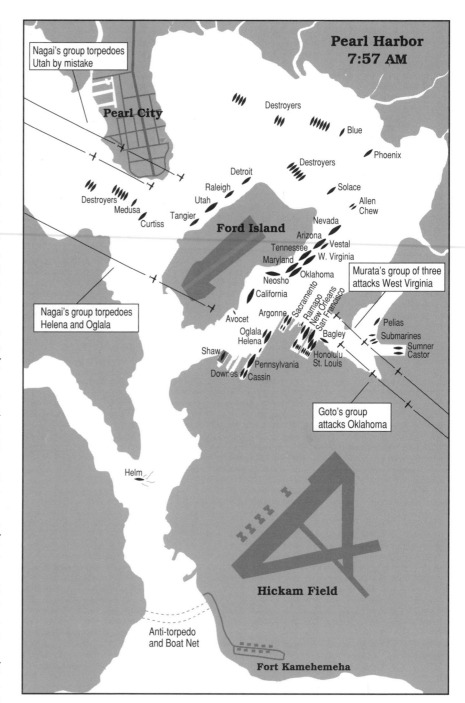

The Japanese torpedo plane attack on Battleship Row was a technical triumph for the Imperial Navy. Standard naval practice dropped torpedoes from 300 feet at a speed of 160 mph. The resulting inertial forces plunged the torpedo to a depth of 100 feet before rising to the surface. Pearl Harbor, however, had an average depth of 40 feet, too shallow for ordinary torpedoes. By 1941, the Japanese found that additional wooden fins, slightly offset in relation to each other reduced the depth of the torpedo's initial dive. Working continuously throughout the year, Japanese researchers finally solved the problem in November. Drop the new torpedoes from a very low altitude and at a slower air speed, and four out of five would sink no deeper than 33 feet and subsequently hit their target.

Battleship Row
(left) as a torpedo hits the USS *Oklahoma.* At 8:00 a.m. the loud-speaker gave the order to man *Oklahoma's* anti-aircraft batteries. Sailors ran for their battle stations amid the sounds of gunfire and explosions from all over the harbor. Within seconds, three torpedoes from Lt. Jinchi Goto's group hit the *Oklahoma.* The ship rapidly listed to 45 degrees. More torpedoes struck the dying vessel on the port side. The crew scrambled over the railing as *Oklahoma* capsized into the mud of Pearl Harbor.

A torpedo strikes
West Virginia in Battleship Row (left). An ensign saw the initial explosions on Ford Island and thought it was an internal fire on the USS *California.* He gave the "Away Fire and Rescue Party" signal. Hundreds of men rushed topside to obey the order and were saved as the first of nine torpedoes slammed into *West Virginia.* The battleship heeled to 25 degrees before counter-flooding corrected the list. *West Virginia* sank on an even keel into Pearl Harbor's debris-filled waters.

Torpedo Attack

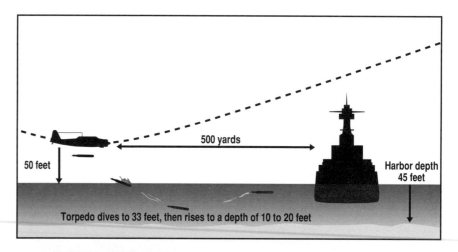

500 yards

50 feet

Harbor depth 45 feet

Torpedo dives to 33 feet, then rises to a depth of 10 to 20 feet

Crewmen on the decks of the great warships in Battleship Row watched what they took to be a Navy exercise as the Japanese torpedo planes roared in. Four groups of torpedo bombers attacked the USS *Oklahoma* in rapid succession. The Japanese observers in the Kate bombers called out *"Atarimashita"* (It struck) when nine torpedoes exploded against the battleship. Tremendous columns of water rose along the *Oklahoma's* side.

Almost simultaneously three groups of torpedo bombers launched on the 38,000 ton *West Virginia*, scoring nine or more hits. Seeing the destruction, two Japanese pilots veered left and torpedoed *California* at the southern end of Battleship Row. Due for inspection on Monday, the *California's* hatches lay open, making the ship especially vulnerable when the torpedoes struck.

Two more torpedo planes angled right to assault USS *Nevada*. Gunners from the destroyer *Bagley* shot down one before it could drop its missile. The second torpedo struck the *Nevada* near the forward turrets.

Meanwhile, five torpedo bombers from the original attack on the cruiser line crossed Ford Island and made a run against the light cruiser *Helena* and a small mine-layer, *Oglala*, moored at the Ten-Ten Dock. Although they dropped five torpedoes, only one struck home. This missile passed underneath the *Oglala* to explode against the *Helena* and flood a large part of the engine room. The pressure wave from the detonation ruptured *Oglala's* hull, and the ship capsized two hours later.

Although the assault happened quickly, the Americans managed to shoot down five of the forty Kate torpedo planes.

The thirty foot hole (above) in USS *California's* port side caused by one of the two torpedoes that struck the ship on December 7th. After salvage the *California* rejoined the fleet and fought in the Marianas.

The target ship USS *Utah* (right) capsizes during the attack on the west side of Ford Island. It was hit by three torpedoes. Fifty-eight sailors lost their lives.

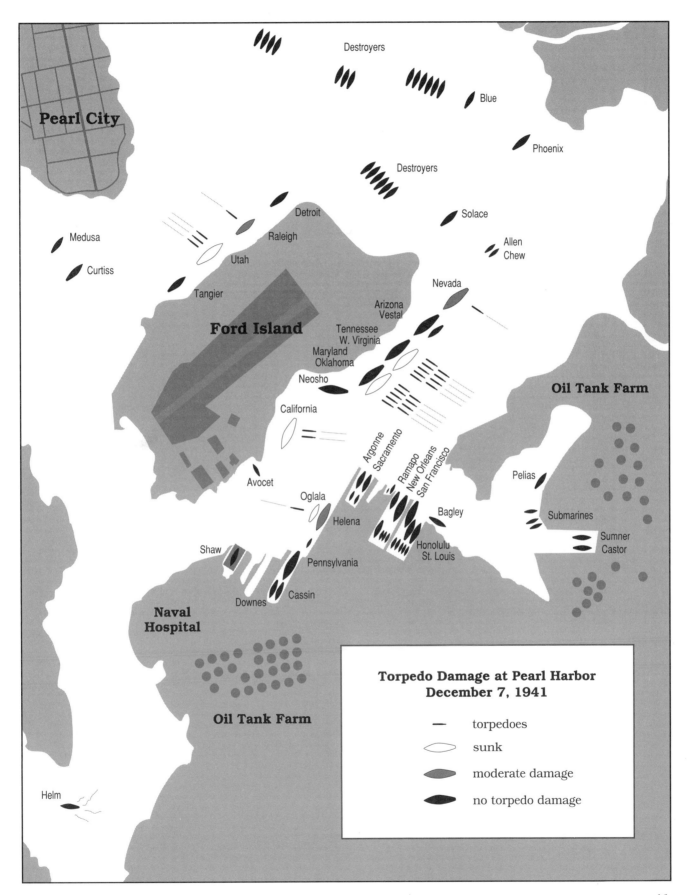

**Torpedo Damage at Pearl Harbor
December 7, 1941**

— torpedoes
⬭ sunk
⬬ moderate damage
⬬ no torpedo damage

Pearl City

Destroyers

Blue

Phoenix

Destroyers

Solace

Medusa

Detroit

Raleigh

Allen
Chew

Curtiss

Utah

Nevada

Tangier

Arizona
Vestal

Ford Island

Tennessee
W. Virginia

Maryland
Oklahoma

Oil Tank Farm

Neosho

California

Argonne
Sacramento

Ramapo
New Orleans
San Francisco

Pelias

Avocet

Oglala

Bagley

Submarines

Helena

Honolulu
St. Louis

Sumner
Castor

Shaw

Pennsylvania

**Naval
Hospital**

Downes   Cassin

Oil Tank Farm

Helm

High-Level Bombing

Fuchida gave the order to attack, *To, to, to* (charge) and his group of 49 high-level bombers swung west of Oahu to approach Pearl Harbor from the south. From 10,000 feet he watched clouds of smoke billow from Hickam Field and Ford Island Naval Air Station as the dive-bombers struck their targets. Far below, columns of water rose against the sides of the battleships—torpedo hits. Fuchida ordered his pilot to bank sharply and the ten groups of planes formed a single column separated by intervals of 600 feet.

When the line of planes reached the mouth of the harbor, American anti-aircraft fire blossomed around them. Each group of Kates headed for Battleship Row to drop their one-ton bombs on a particular warship. Fuchida's squadron aimed for USS *Nevada* at the north end of Ford Island, but clouds obscured the ship at the last moment. His four aircraft banked right toward Honolulu to circle back for another try.

Other sections made their bombing runs, and as Fuchida turned back to Pearl Harbor a tremendous explosion shook Battleship Row. His plane trembled from the shock wave and a huge column of dark red smoke rose a thousand feet into the air. Through his binoculars Fuchida saw the flame and red smoke erupt together, and realized the powder magazines on the USS *Arizona* had exploded.

He continued the run, and his planes dropped their four bombs on the USS *Maryland*. The bombs disappeared toward their target and he saw two tiny flashes, but the bombs missed the moored battleship. Fuchida's plane remained over the harbor to direct operations. Circling above Battleship Row, he noted with satisfaction four battleships sunk and three damaged.

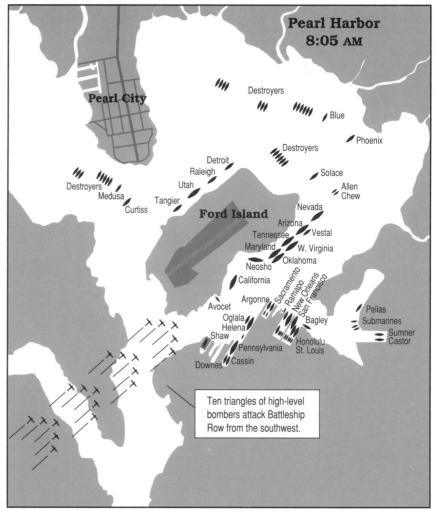

Pearl Harbor 8:05 AM

Pearl City

Destroyers

Blue

Phoenix

Destroyers

Detroit
Raleigh
Solace

Destroyers
Allen Chew
Medusa
Utah
Nevada
Curtiss
Tangier
Ford Island
Arizona
Tennessee
Vestal
Maryland
W. Virginia
Neosho
Oklahoma
California
Sacramento
Argonne
Ramapo
New Orleans
San Francisco
Pelias
Submarines
Avocet
Oglala
Bagley
Helena
Sumner
Castor
Shaw
Honolulu
Pennsylvania
St. Louis
Downes
Cassin

Ten triangles of high-level bombers attack Battleship Row from the southwest.

42

This captured Japanese photograph was taken from a Kate high-level bomber at the beginning of the bombing attack on Battleship Row. At the extreme right the USS *Nevada* is covered with smoke. Directly in front of it is the *Arizona's* stern. Two splashes mark a near miss and a bomb hit aft. Forward of *Arizona,* oil gushes out of the USS *West Virginia* and the USS *Oklahoma* (further forward). The *Oklahoma* has just been struck by a torpedo amidships and is beginning to capsize.

Another captured Japanese photograph of Battleship Row, this picture was taken five minutes later. At the right, smoke has cleared from the USS *Nevada* which is listing from a torpedo hit in the bow. To the left, a column of smoke pours from the forward section of *Arizona* just after the front 14-inch gun magazines detonated. Further left, the sterns of the *Tennessee* and the listing *West Virginia* are visible through the smoke. Over 1,100 sailors aboard *Arizona* lost their lives.

Loss of the Arizona

In 1906 the British Navy created the first modern battleship, the revolutionary HMS *Dreadnought*. This 17,000 ton warship had centralized fire control, a main battery of ten 12-inch guns, and fast, more reliable turbine engines. It could easily sink any naval vessel built before it.

The *Dreadnought* set off a tremendous arms race between Great Britain, Germany, Japan, and the United States. Seven years later, as part of that competition, the U.S. Navy's General Board ordered two Pennsylvania-class battleships to match the capabilities of two new Japanese warships.

The U.S. ships, *Pennsylvania* and *Arizona*, were designed to carry twelve 14-inch guns in four triple turrets, have a top speed of 21 knots, a cruising range of 7,000 miles, and be powered by oil instead of coal.

Construction of the *Arizona* began at the Brooklyn Navy Yard in March 1914. Six months after the United States entered World War I, the ship finished its sea trials and was commissioned into the U.S. Navy. The *Arizona* spent its first year with the Atlantic Fleet assigned to gunnery training.

After the Armistice (November 1918), the new battleship accompanied the British Grand Fleet on maneuvers for three months. The British were impressed with *Arizona*, and *Jane's Fighting Ships* praised the battleship for its steady handling, good seagoing characteristics, and excellent long-range gunnery. Three years later, in 1921, the *Arizona* joined the U.S. Pacific Fleet in San Pedro, California. Except for an eighteen month modernization in the early 1930s at the Norfolk, Virginia Navy Yard, the battleship spent the rest of its active service with the Pacific Fleet.

USS Arizona

Commissioned: October 1917
Length Overall: 608 feet
Width: 97 feet (beam)
Mean Draft: 29 feet
Displacement: 32,500 tons
Battery: twelve 14-inch guns
Armor: main belt 13.5 inches
   turrets 9–18 inches
   conning tower 16 inches
Aircraft: 3 OS2U Kingfishers
Range: (after modernization)
   8,500 miles at 20 knots
   13,000 miles at 15 knots
Fuel Oil Capacity: 4,630 tons
Crew: 1,731 men
Total Cost: $12,993,000

Three decks (the main, second, and third) extended the full length of the ship. *Arizona* had two platform decks below the third deck in the forward and aft turret areas. The battleship mounted its twelve 14-inch rifles in four triple turrets. Each gun could fire a 1,400 lb. armor-piercing shell twenty miles. The shell handling rooms carried approximately 100 rounds per gun. Three magazines on each side of the ship's first platform deck held over fifty tons of smokeless powder.

Rear Admiral Isaac C. Kidd

In the pre-war battleship Navy, many officers and men spent their entire careers aboard the same ship. Rear Admiral Kidd, commander of Battleship Division One, flew his flag in *Arizona*. He had previously served as captain of the *Arizona* from 1938 to early 1940. During the attack on Pearl Harbor he was last seen alive on *Arizona's* signal bridge.

Franklin Van Valkenburgh

became captain of the *Arizona* in February 1941. At the start of the attack, he joined other officers on the navigation bridge. Seconds later, the magazine detonation blew out the bridge windows and filled the compartment with flames. The captain and the quartermaster tried to escape through a port door, but failed to reach safety before flames surrounded them.

The *Arizona* at sea during a 1930 visit by President Herbert Hoover. In 1929, the U.S. Navy modernized *Arizona* at a cost of $5,290,000. Major changes included thicker deck armor to protect against aerial bombs, larger fuel capacity, a heavier anti-aircraft battery, and increased torpedo protection. These improvements prepared *Arizona* for battle against the Japanese Navy. Ironically, the *Arizona* never fought Japanese ships, but instead fell victim to a new weapon of war: carrier-borne aircraft.

Battleship Row 8:00 AM

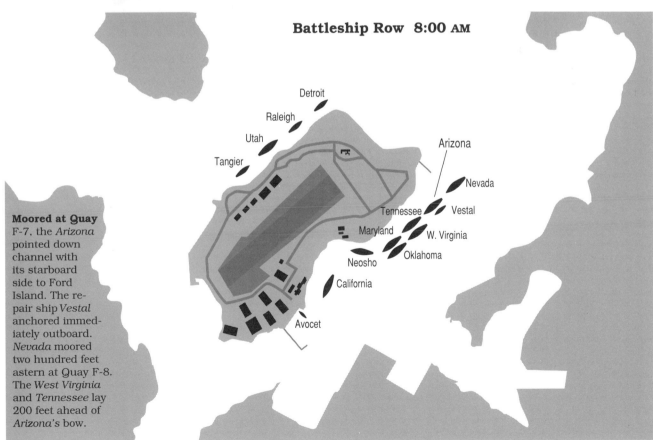

Detroit
Raleigh
Utah
Tangier
Arizona
Nevada
Tennessee
Vestal
Maryland
W. Virginia
Oklahoma
Neosho
California
Avocet

Moored at Quay F-7, the *Arizona* pointed down channel with its starboard side to Ford Island. The repair ship *Vestal* anchored immediately outboard. *Nevada* moored two hundred feet astern at Quay F-8. The *West Virginia* and *Tennessee* lay 200 feet ahead of *Arizona*'s bow.

Loss of the Arizona

USS *Arizona* was tied up at Quay F-7 alongside Ford Island on the morning of December 7, 1941. Just before 8 a.m., while a Marine Honor Guard waited on *Arizona's* stern for the signal to hoist the Stars and Stripes, some of the men noticed planes, approaching from several directions. Within seconds they heard the first bombs fall on the seaplane station at Ford Island. The marines hurriedly raised the flag and ran for their battle stations.

Dozens of men watched incredulously as Kate torpedo planes attacked the *Oklahoma* and *West Virginia*, a few hundred feet away. Others saw high-level bombers making runs from the south.

Someone sounded the ship's air raid alarm just before Capt. Van Valkenburgh ordered General Quarters and went to the bridge. Moments later, the first bomb struck *Arizona* astern near Turret No. 4. Two more bombs exploded on the aft quarterdeck. The adjacent repair ship, *Vestal*, also took two direct hits. Rear Admiral Kidd went to *Arizona's* signal bridge, while Captain Van Valkenburgh, along with the quartermaster and an ensign, directed the fight from the navigation bridge.

The next brace of bombs hit forward. The quartermaster had just reported a bomb explosion near Turret No. 2 when the forward magazines detonated. Sailors, clinging to the capsizing battleship *Oklahoma*, saw a terrific blast and felt the force of the explosion move upward. *Arizona* shook violently, its foremast keeled over, and flames engulfed the ship.

From the nearby *Vestal*, sailors could see men on the *Arizona*, walking on deck and burning alive. Within a few seconds they fell dead, as the blazing *Arizona* sank to the floor of Pearl Harbor.

USS *Arizona* and the repair ship USS *Vestal* lay next to last in Battleship Row when Fuchida's forty-nine Kate bombers attacked from the south. Each Kate carried a 1,760 pound, 16-inch armor-piercing naval shell which had been converted to an aerial bomb. Two groups dropped their bombs on the *Arizona* and scored four hits. One bomb damaged the port air intakes and forced a tremendous smoke column from the stack. The second shell hit the upper deck beside Turret No. 2. Seconds later, the ship's forward magazines detonated. The U.S. Navy's Bureau of Ships later analyzed the disaster and determined the probable sequence of events. The bomb near the second turret pierced the main and second levels, passed through the crew's quarters there, and exploded on the third armored deck. This five-inch steel deck lay immediately over the 14-inch powder magazines. Somehow, the explosion ruptured the forward oil tanks and caused an intense fire around *Arizona's* two front turrets. Near those turrets, on the third deck, five

Forward Turrets of Arizona
First Platform

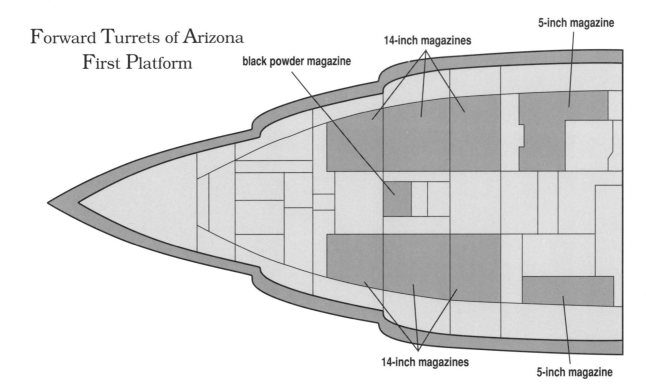

black powder magazine

14-inch magazines

5-inch magazine

14-inch magazines

5-inch magazine

Bomb Hit on Arizona's Forward Magazines

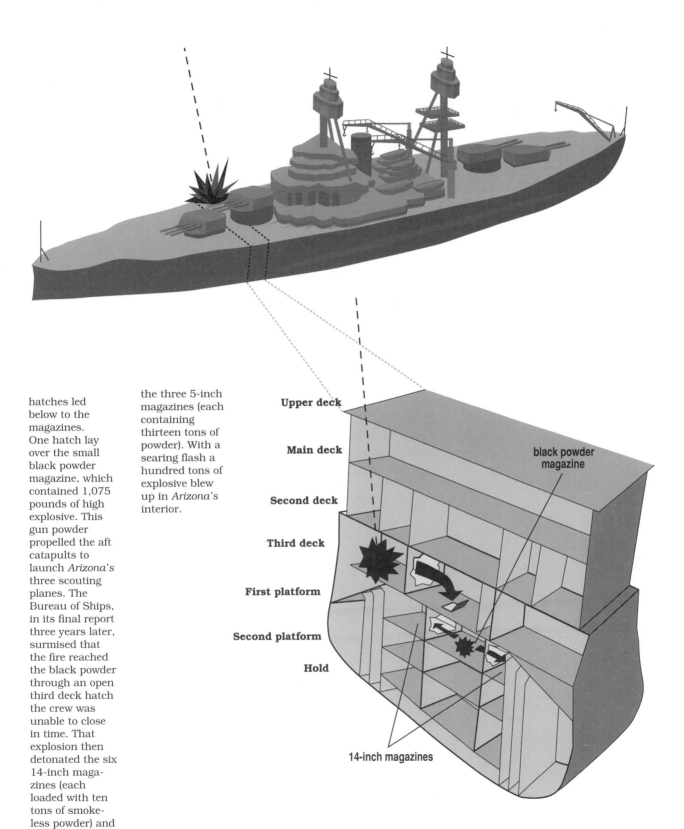

hatches led below to the magazines. One hatch lay over the small black powder magazine, which contained 1,075 pounds of high explosive. This gun powder propelled the aft catapults to launch *Arizona's* three scouting planes. The Bureau of Ships, in its final report three years later, surmised that the fire reached the black powder through an open third deck hatch the crew was unable to close in time. That explosion then detonated the six 14-inch magazines (each loaded with ten tons of smokeless powder) and the three 5-inch magazines (each containing thirteen tons of powder). With a searing flash a hundred tons of explosive blew up in *Arizona's* interior.

Upper deck

Main deck

Second deck

Third deck

First platform

Second platform

Hold

black powder magazine

14-inch magazines

Loss of the Arizona

In a remarkable film sequence, an amateur movie cameraman on Ford Island photographed the destruction of the USS *Arizona*. The time was approximately 8:05 a.m. In the first frame, *Arizona* is in the foreground and the repair ship *Vestal* lies behind it. The bow of the battleship *Nevada* is on the left. Faint traces of smoke are from fires that started when a bomb struck the *Vestal*. *West Virginia*'s listing masts are visible forward of *Arizona*.

The second frame, taken two seconds after a bomb hit near *Arizona's* Turret No. 2, shows an explosion and resulting oil fire. *Arizona* normally carried 4,600 tons of fuel, distributed in tanks inside the hull of the ship.

This fire grows in intensity in the third frame. By the fourth frame, fire engulfs the warship's entire forward section. A jet of black smoke shoots up from *Arizona's* funnel. This discharge gave rise to the story that a bomb went down the ship's stack. Actually, the bomb damaged the adjacent air intakes, and incomplete boiler combustion caused the smoke.

Frame five captures the beginning of the fatal magazine explosion. The tremendous force of this blast hurled the forward half of *Arizona's* internal structure into Pearl Harbor. Debris from the battleship, including the arms, legs, and heads of men showered down on nearby ships.

Frame seven captures the end of the magazine explosion and the beginning of the massive oil fire which consumed the wrecked vessel's fuel supply. The catastrophe occurred in approximately seven seconds. A few hundred men in the aft part of the ship survived; most of the crew perished. The *Arizona* continued to burn for two days—until Tuesday afternoon.

1

4

7

2

3

5

6

8

9

Loss of the Arizona

At 10:00 a.m. the last Japanese planes disappeared northward and a stunned Pacific Fleet surveyed the damage. Battleship Row was wrecked. The *Oklahoma* lay capsized, the *West Virginia* sat with its decks flooded and its port side blown away, and the twisted hull of *Arizona* burned. Bodies littered the harbor. On the stern of the USS *Arizona*, Lieutenant Commander Fuqua, assisted by uninjured crewmen, managed to transfer one hundred wounded sailors to the hospital ship, *Solace*. He was awarded the Congressional Medal of Honor for his courageous actions that morning.

Other small boats braved the burning oil and picked up loads of dazed men. Most of the survivors were covered with oil and many were badly burned. Thirty years later in an interview, a rescuer wept when he recalled being covered with oil, water, burned flesh, and blood.

The Navy established that 1,177 of *Arizona's* crew of 1,731 went down with the ship. Among the dead were Captain Franklin Van Valkenburgh and Rear Admiral Isaac Kidd, Commander of Battleship Division One. The destruction of the *Arizona* was the worst single naval disaster in American history.

Rescue crews removed everyone left alive from the *Arizona*, which continued to burn while the fire consumed its 4,000 tons of fuel oil. Aboard the repair ship *Vestal,* now beached a safe distance away, an officer surveyed debris blown onto the deck from the battleship's explosion. He found part of an *Arizona* crewman's locker, which contained a letter the young sailor had been writing to his mother the night before the attack. It ended " I am going to turn in now, Mother, I'll finish this tomorrow."

Damage to the Arizona

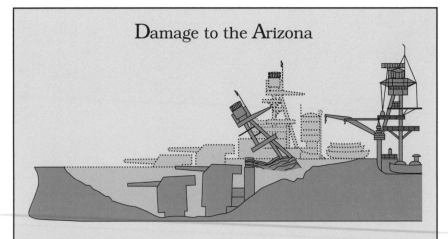

In October 1944 the Pearl Harbor Navy Yard sent its final war damage report on the USS *Arizona* to the chief of the Bureau of Ships. Based on extensive underwater surveys it told the following: the explosion in the forward magazines vented through the sides of the ship from about frame 10 to frame 70, and upward through the decks forward of Turret No. 1. Turret No. 1, with its barbette, fell approximately 22 feet as the supporting decks were blown away. Turret No. 2, with its barbette, fell 23 feet. The rest of the ship's structure above the top edge of the side armor (the upper, main, and second decks) between frames 10 and 70 was completely demolished; in fact, most of it was missing. The armor belt remained substantially in place. Short pieces of the hull projected outward horizontally on both sides. *Arizona's* foremast collapsed when the port leg of this mast's tripod failed during the explosion and the starboard leg was insufficient to stop its fall. Given the intense damage to the forward part of the ship, the Pearl Harbor Navy Yard concluded its report by recommending no further salvage work.

A clock (left) salvaged from the *Arizona*. It stopped at 8:05 a.m. just before the ship's magazines detonated.

The *Arizona* (above) burns in the late morning on December 7, 1941. Rescue parties found Admiral Kidd's charred body on the boat deck at the foot of the bridge ladder. They did not find Captain Van Valkenburgh's body. However, a few days after the attack, a search party noticed a pile of human ashes on the boat deck near the bridge. In the cremated remains they discovered a Naval Academy ring with the engraved name of Franklin Van Valkenburgh. The U.S. government posthumously awarded Admiral Kidd and Captain Van Valkenburgh the Congressional Medal of Honor.

Research after the war credited the hits on or near *Arizona's* stern to one of the groups of Kate bombers *(buntai)* from the *Kaga.* A *buntai* from the *Hiryu,* led by Lt. Comdr. Tadashi Kusumi, dropped the fatal bomb which detonated the *Arizona's* forward magazines.

The wreck of the USS *Arizona* (right) photographed from the bow on December 10th.

Ford Island Naval Air Station

In 1923 the U.S. Navy built a runway and a seaplane base on Ford Island. In the late 1930s the government added a supply depot and expanded the base to a naval air station. Carrier aircraft landed on the mile-long island when their ships were in port.

At 7:55 a.m. on December 7th, Lieutenant Commander Logan Ramsey, operations officer of Patrol Wing Two, heard a dive-bomber's scream. He thought it was a Navy pilot grandstanding until an explosion rocked the hangar area. Ramsey rushed across the hall of the Command Center to the radio room and told the radio operators to send out the uncoded message: "Air Raid Pearl Harbor. This is not drill."

Even as the message went out Val dive-bombers from the Japanese carrier *Shokaku* continued to bomb and strafe the seaplane hangars. Hangar No. 6 and its ramp took at least five bomb hits. Hangar 38 suffered minor damage from near misses. Later in the raid a 550 lb. bomb smashed into the courtyard of the medical dispensary but caused no injuries.

Hundreds of casualties from the torpedo and bombing attack on Battleship Row poured into Ford Island's first aid stations. So many wounded arrived that the doctors only had time to give them morphine, and move on. The fire brigade attempted to put out the fires at the seaplane hangars, but the *Arizona* had sunk on the island's water mains which ran under its berth, and there was no water pressure.

Ford Island received one major piece of luck on December 7th. During the second wave, nine high-level bombers assigned to strike the base became disoriented in the smoke above the harbor and missed the naval air station entirely.

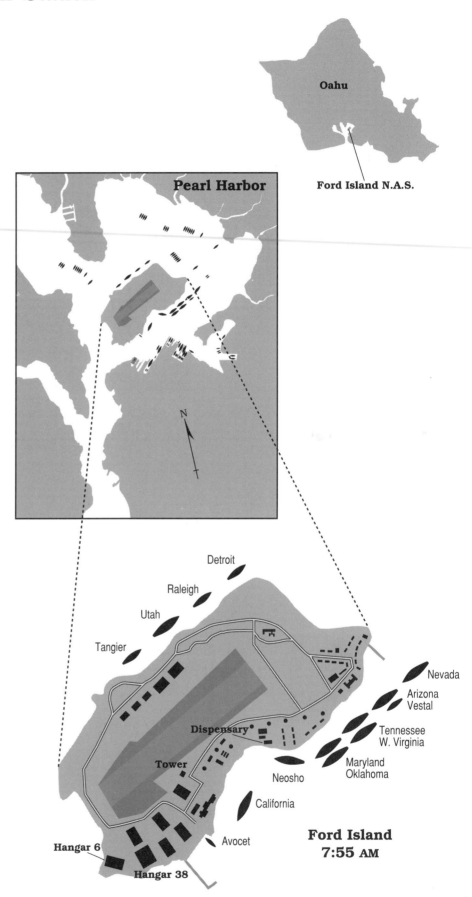

Oahu

Ford Island N.A.S.

Pearl Harbor

N

Detroit

Raleigh

Utah

Tangier

Dispensary

Tower

Hangar 6

Hangar 38

Nevada

Arizona
Vestal

Tennessee
W. Virginia

Maryland
Oklahoma

Neosho

California

Avocet

**Ford Island
7:55 AM**

Ford Island NAS
Seaplane Base
(above) mid-
morning on
December 7th.
The men of Patrol
Squadrons VP 22,
VP 23 and VP24
looked forward to
a routine Sunday
of maintenance
and repair after
a hard week of
training. Earlier
in the week they
had patrolled
400 miles to the
north and north-
west of Oahu,
the most likely
line of approach
of an enemy task
force. Now they
had an oppor-
tunity to work on
the new PBY-5s
which had just
replaced some of
the obsolete PBY-
3s. Armor and
self-sealing gas
tanks were being
installed on each
plane. They
worked on Sunday
because experi-
enced personnel
were in short
supply. Squadrons
sent 10% of their
newly trained
flight crews back
to the U.S. every
three months to
form new units.

Bomb crater
(left) in the Ford
Island dispensary
courtyard.

53

Hickam Field—First Wave

Normally quiet on a Sunday morning, Hickam Field expected a flight of twelve B-17s from California at 8 a.m., and numerous flight crews prepared for the bombers' arrival. Completed in 1940, Hickam Field was home to 12 B-17s, 33 obsolete B-18s, and 12 A-20 attack bombers. Following General Short's first stage alert order, the 18th Bombardment Wing lined up its planes in four rows about ten feet apart.

A little before 8 a.m. the airmen heard the first planes attacking Battleship Row and Ford Island Naval Air Station. Within seconds, nine dive-bombers from carrier *Shokaku* swept in from the northeast and blasted buildings and hangars. Eight more Vals bombed the hangar line from the southwest, while nine Zeros from *Akagi* strafed the parked planes.

Japanese dive-bombers scored direct hits on the repair hangar, base chapel, enlisted men's beer hall, guardhouse, and firehouse. A bomb smashed into the enlisted men's mess hall and killed thirty-five men as they ate breakfast. Another bomb killed twenty-two men who were preparing B-18s for a training flight.

A young radio operator saw an airman running down the hangar line pursed by a strafing Zero. Inexplicably the man was getting shorter as he ran. It took the radioman a few seconds before he realized in horror the airman's legs had been shot off. Within fifteen minutes Hickam Field was reduced to a blazing wreck.

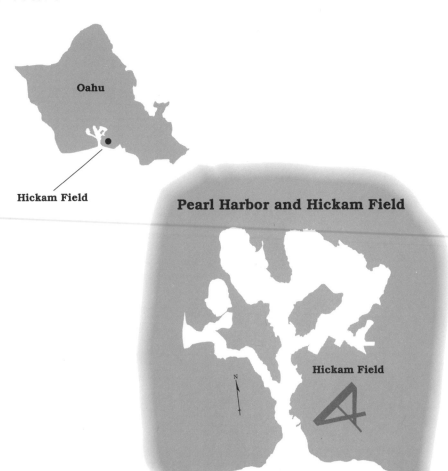

Pearl Harbor and Hickam Field

The embattled American flag (right) flies over Hickam Field later in the raid. Bombed Halemakai Barracks burns in the background. Hickam Field's name honored Lieutenant Colonel Horace Hickam, a distinguished pilot and army aviation pioneer who was killed in an aircraft accident at Ft. Crockett, Texas in 1934.

54

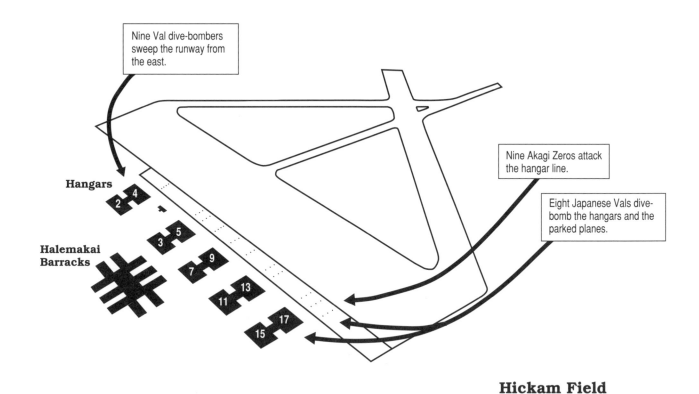

Nine Val dive-bombers sweep the runway from the east.

Nine Akagi Zeros attack the hangar line.

Eight Japanese Vals dive-bomb the hangars and the parked planes.

Hangars

Halemakai Barracks

**Hickam Field
7:55 AM**

Wheeler Field—First Wave

Wheeler Field, the main U.S. Army Air Force fighter base on Oahu, was home to the 14th Pursuit Wing. One hundred and forty fighters were stationed at the field—87 modern P-40s and the rest obsolete P-36 and P-26 types. Although Wheeler lacked anti-aircraft guns and air raid shelters, 125 protective bunkers—U-shaped earthen walls eight feet high—had been constructed to protect the aircraft from strafing and bombs.

The base commander, Colonel William Flood objected to General Short's November 27th order to remove the planes from their bunkers and line them up along the hangars. He asked permission to keep the fighters sheltered, but was refused on the grounds that it would alarm the local population.

At 7:51 a.m. on December 7th 25 Val dive-bombers destroyed most of Oahu's fighter strength.

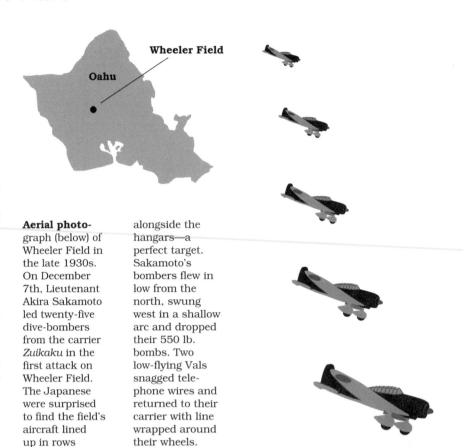

Aerial photograph (below) of Wheeler Field in the late 1930s. On December 7th, Lieutenant Akira Sakamoto led twenty-five dive-bombers from the carrier *Zuikaku* in the first attack on Wheeler Field. The Japanese were surprised to find the field's aircraft lined up in rows alongside the hangars—a perfect target. Sakamoto's bombers flew in low from the north, swung west in a shallow arc and dropped their 550 lb. bombs. Two low-flying Vals snagged telephone wires and returned to their carrier with line wrapped around their wheels.

Wheeler Field 7:51 AM

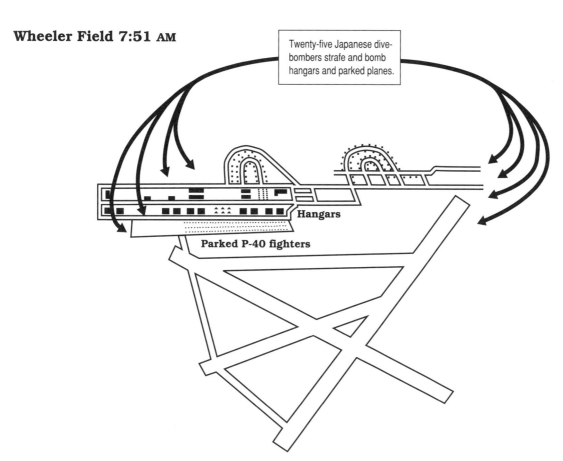

Twenty-five Japanese dive-bombers strafe and bomb hangars and parked planes.

Hangars

Parked P-40 fighters

A captured Japanese photograph (below) of Wheeler Field under attack. A number of hangars and dozens of planes are burning. Val dive-bombers hit the hangars, destroyed the base PX, and attacked the fire-house. Zero fighters followed, and strafed the base and adjacent residential areas. No Japanese planes were shot down during this raid on Wheeler Field.

Kaneohe Naval Air Station—First Wave

In December 1941, contractors were busy working on the new Kaneohe Naval Air Station on the Mokapu Peninsula. Although construction continued on the landing mat and utility connections, Kaneohe was an operating base. With the barracks, administration building, and two hangars completed, 334 officers and enlisted men, and a contingent of 95 marines manned the patrol plane station.

Kaneohe housed the thirty-six PBY-5 seaplanes of Patrol Wing One. The wing consisted of three squadrons: VP 11, VP 12, and VP 14, each with twelve planes. Like other airfields on Oahu, the base lacked dedicated anti-aircraft guns.

On the morning of December 7th, three of Kaneohe's PBY-5s patrolled south of Oahu, four moored in the bay a thousand yards apart, four sat in Hangar One, and the remaining twenty-five aircraft parked on the station's ramp. A ready-duty plane and a crew of thirty men stood hangar watch.

At 7:53 a.m. eleven Japanese Zeros approached from the north and strafed Kaneohe's PBYs with machine guns and 20 mm cannon fire. Instantly, the peaceful air station became a scene from Dante's *Inferno*. Seaplanes on the ramp and in the water erupted in flames. A car exploded and burned when a Zero's bullets hit its gas tank. Men ran in all directions to get guns and ammunition from their planes and to set up anti-aircraft fire. Officers shouted orders while bullets ricocheted off the hangars.

Incredibly, the first attack lasted only eight minutes and the Japanese Zeros departed without loss. Every exposed PBY at Kaneohe was damaged or on fire—only the three planes on patrol escaped.

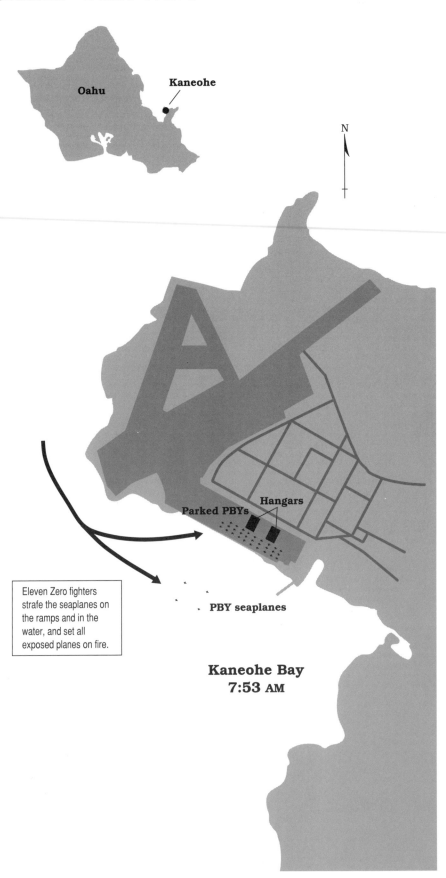

Oahu

Kaneohe

N

Parked PBYs

Hangars

Eleven Zero fighters strafe the seaplanes on the ramps and in the water, and set all exposed planes on fire.

PBY seaplanes

**Kaneohe Bay
7:53 AM**

A Kate bomber (above) flies over Kaneohe Naval Air Station.

The PBY patrol bomber (right) was the best reconnaissance seaplane of World War II. Also known by its Royal Air Force name, "Catalina," this versatile aircraft was first ordered by the U.S. Navy in 1936. By December 7, 1941, 424 PBYs were in service with the Fleet. The Catalina's two 1,200 HP Pratt & Whitney engines gave it a speed of 190 miles per hour, a maximum ceiling of 24,000 feet, and a very long range of 4,000 miles. The PBY effectively performed patrol, anti-submarine, and search and rescue roles throughout the war. Japanese carrier planes destroyed 33 of Kaneohe's 36 PBYs during the attack.

Ewa Marine Corps Air Station—First Wave

As part of United States military expansion in the Pacific, the Marine Corps established Ewa Field near the southwestern tip of Oahu. In late 1941 the air station included a five thousand foot runway, several groups of large tents, some permanent wooden buildings, and an unused dirigible mooring mast.

Forty-eight planes were stationed at Ewa, most of them new SBD dive-bombers or F4F fighters. These planes made up three squadrons of the 21st Marine Aircraft Group. They represented a threat to any attacker, and the Japanese raiders marked them for destruction.

At 7:53 a.m. on December 7th, Ewa's officer of the day, Captain Leonard Ashwell, looked up and saw a line of 18 torpedo planes, heading for Pearl Harbor. Even

as he realized they were Japanese, six Zero fighters flew in over the base from the northwest and began to strafe the aircraft which sat in rows on the runway.

A low-flying Zero machine-gunned the car of base commander Lieutenant Colonel Claude Larkin while he drove toward Ewa Field. The quick-thinking officer dived into a nearby ditch and escaped injury, only to be wounded by shrapnel later in the attack. At the base, one of the firemen attempted to drive his vehicle to the flight line to combat the fires. Strafing Zeros shot out the truck's rear tires, and the brave marine wisely took

cover behind some crates. Fire fighters had more success in putting out the flames that threatened the hospital and its adjacent medical stores.

Altogether, 30 Zeros and many Val dive-bombers strafed Ewa Field during the attack. By 8:15, two-thirds of Ewa's aircraft were in flames.

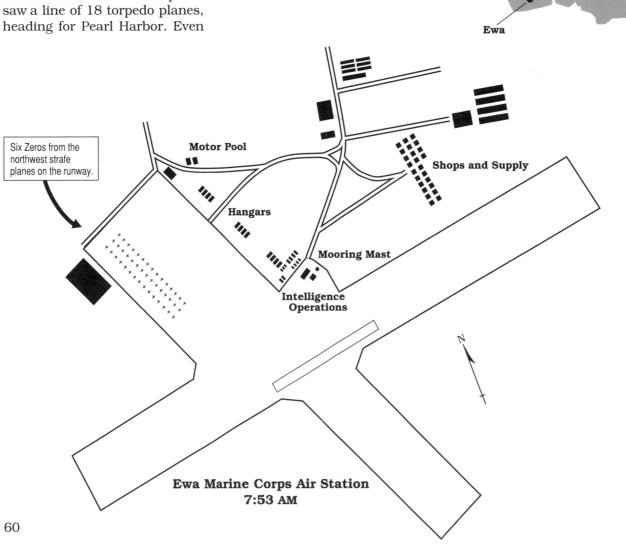

Six Zeros from the northwest strafe planes on the runway.

Motor Pool

Hangars

Shops and Supply

Mooring Mast

Intelligence Operations

Oahu

Ewa

**Ewa Marine Corps Air Station
7:53 AM**

Ewa Marine
Corps Air Station
(above) before the
attack. Planes in
the foreground
are obsolete
SB2U Vindicator
dive-bombers.
Ewa also had
twenty-three new
Dauntless SBD
dive-bombers.
These versatile
Navy planes were
to prove their
worth at the
battle of Midway.
More than 5,300
were built during
the war.

A civilian car
(right) destroyed
by Japanese
strafing during
the attack.

Bellows Field—First Wave

Located southeast of Kaneohe, Bellows Field became a permanent Army Air Force base in July 1941. Named in honor of World War I hero, Lt. Franklin Bellows, the airfield expanded rapidly to provide increased pilot training. Lt. Col. Leonard Weddington assumed his eventful command of Bellows' 409 officers and enlisted men in late October 1941.

On December 7th, twelve P-40 fighters from the 44th Pursuit Squadron, and nine reconnaissance (O-47) planes from the 86th Observation Squadron parked in single file along the runway at fifteen-foot intervals. The P-40s had finished a week of aerial gunnery practice on Saturday, and following standard procedure, flight crews removed the planes' machine guns for cleaning the next morning.

At 8:30 a.m. that Sunday, while the men ate breakfast and prepared for church, a single Japanese fighter roared in from the sea and strafed the tent area. After one pass—perhaps out of ammunition—the Zero flew back toward Kaneohe. Its bullets wounded one of the camp's sergeants. This critical warning gave Bellows airmen a chance to disperse some of their planes before the Japanese returned a half hour later.

Flying in three V-formations, eight Zeros from the carrier *Hiryu* attacked Bellows Field. For fifteen minutes the planes strafed the base with machine guns and 20 mm cannon fire. Two O-47 reconnaissance planes were damaged and a gasoline truck destroyed. The Japanese shot down three American P-40s when they attempted to take off.

Lacking heavier anti-aircraft guns, U.S. airmen fought back with rifles and machine guns salvaged from the planes, but did not bring down any Zeros.

U.S. Aircraft

The B-17

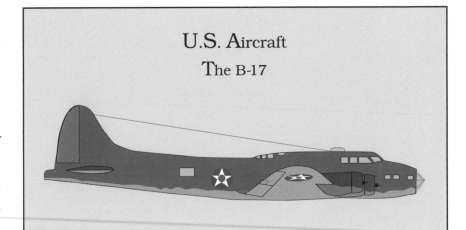

In the early 1930s the U.S. Army Air Corps became interested in building a heavy long-range bomber. The Boeing Aircraft Company in Seattle took up the challenge and its experimental B-17 (model 299) flew in July 1935. The multiple machine gun emplacements quickly won the plane its immortal nickname, the Flying Fortress. Boeing manufactured a total of 12,731 B-17s of all types between 1935 and 1945.

More than 4,700 were lost on combat missions.

Wing:	103 feet 9 inches
Length:	73 feet 10 inches
Weight:	33,279 lbs. (empty)
	40,260 lbs. (loaded)
Speed:	226 mph (cruising)
	317 mph (max.)
Ceiling:	35,000 feet
Range:	3,300 miles
Guns:	Nine 50 caliber
	machine guns
Crew:	10 men

The P-40

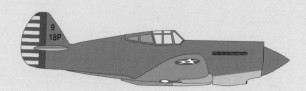

In the late 1930s the Curtiss Aircraft Company offered a new fighter design, the P-40, to the U.S. Army Air Corps. After development and prototype testing the Army approved the model, and in January 1939 placed an order for 524 planes. The P-40 served in all theaters of World War II and excelled as a ground support aircraft. It achieved lasting fame as the main fighter of General Claire

Chennault's China-based "Flying Tigers" from 1941 through 1942.

Wingspan:	37 feet 4 inches
Length:	31 feet 2 inches
Weight:	6,300 lbs. (empty)
	9,250 lbs. (loaded)
Speed:	300 mph (cruising)
	354 mph (max.)
Ceiling:	29,000 feet
Range:	700 miles
Guns:	six 50 caliber
	machine guns

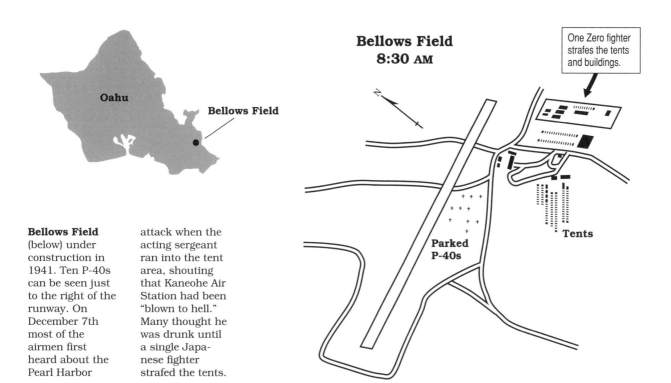

Oahu

Bellows Field

Bellows Field
8:30 AM

One Zero fighter strafes the tents and buildings.

N

Parked P-40s

Tents

Bellows Field (below) under construction in 1941. Ten P-40s can be seen just to the right of the runway. On December 7th most of the airmen first heard about the Pearl Harbor attack when the acting sergeant ran into the tent area, shouting that Kaneohe Air Station had been "blown to hell." Many thought he was drunk until a single Japanese fighter strafed the tents.

They Arrived During the Fight

On the evening of December 6, 1941 thirteen B-17s left Hamilton Field in northern California to reinforce the U.S. air command in the Philippines. They planned to refuel on Oahu the next morning. Although one plane developed engine trouble and turned back, twelve aircraft continued the fourteen hour flight to Hickam Field. In Hawaii, the Army Air Force arranged to have radio station KGMB broadcast all night so the bombers could home in on the signal. The B-17s arrived over Hickam Field Sunday morning about 8:20 a.m. and found themselves in the middle of a desperate battle.

Stripped of armor and ammunition to achieve maximum range, the planes became another target for the attacking Zeros. Japanese fighters jumped the first two B-17s that flew into Hickam. Twenty mm cannon shells ignited flames aboard one of the planes and it burned in half on the runway. Bullets wounded several men in the second bomber, and the pilot crash landed the plane at Bellows Field.

Two B-17s escaped the destruction that swirled around Hickam and managed to land at tiny 1,200-foot Haleiwa Field. Another of the big four-engine planes set down on Kahuku Golf Course on northern Oahu.

Meanwhile, Task Force 8, on its way back from Wake Island, reached a point two hundred miles west of Oahu. Acting on recent war warnings, its commander, Admiral Halsey, in the aircraft carrier *Enterprise,* sent up eighteen scout planes at 6:15 a.m. He ordered them to reconnoiter a 180-degree sector in front of the ship, then land at Ford Island. The scouts flew in over Pearl Harbor in time to lose five planes to the Japanese and a sixth to U.S. anti-aircraft fire.

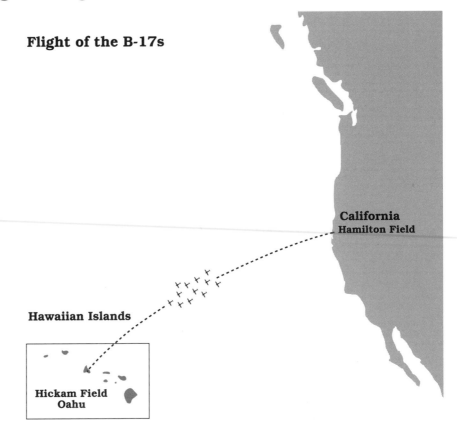

Flight of the B-17s

California
Hickam Field

Hawaiian Islands

Hickam Field
Oahu

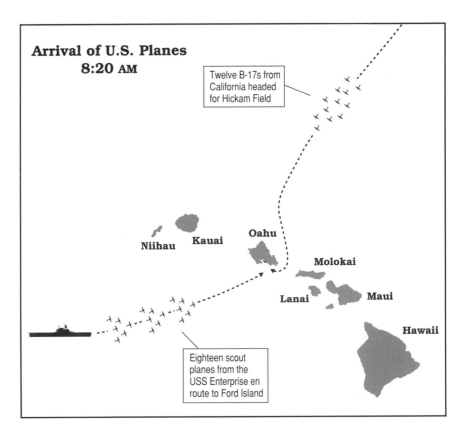

**Arrival of U.S. Planes
8:20 AM**

Twelve B-17s from California headed for Hickam Field

Niihau Kauai Oahu

Molokai

Lanai Maui

Hawaii

Eighteen scout planes from the USS Enterprise en route to Ford Island

Japanese Val dive-bombers (above) photographed from one of the twelve B-17s arriving at Hickam Field. The only fatality suffered by the B-17s occurred when the tenth bomber came into Hickam. A Japanese cannon shell exploded some magnesium flares in the B-17's radio compartment, and the plane caught fire and broke in two as it bounced down on the runway. The crew ran for shelter, but a strafing Zero killed the flight surgeon, William Schick. Three months later, on his birthday, his widow gave birth to his son, William Schick.

Lt. Robert Richards' B-17 (right) after skidding off the short runway at Bellows Field in an emergency landing.

Midget Submarine Attack

The Americans had their first contact with the five Japanese midget submarines of the Special Attack Force at 6:45 a.m. The destroyer USS *Ward* shelled and sank one midget sub as it trailed a small cargo ship into the harbor. The tiny submarine went down in 1,000 feet of water, and gave the American Navy the first victory of the upcoming battle.

A large anti-submarine net protected the entrance to Pearl Harbor. Unfortunately, after admitting two mine sweepers at 5 a.m., the Navy crew failed to close the net, and at least one midget sub entered the harbor.

At 8:30 a.m., while the first wave aircraft attack was ending, the destroyer *Zane* sighted a midget submarine 200 yards astern of the USS *Medusa*. The seaplane tender *Curtiss* spotted the sub at the same time and opened fire. The midget launched a torpedo, but it missed the ships and exploded harmlessly against the shore.

Meanwhile, the USS *Monaghan* came up and rammed the sub at full speed. The small vessel rolled under the destroyer's stern, and the *Monaghan* dropped depth charges. Just before it sank, the submarine fired its second torpedo, but missed.

The third midget sub suffered from a defective gyroscope and repeatedly ran aground on various reefs when it attempted to enter the harbor. It finally lost battery power, drifted around the island, and washed ashore near Bellows Field the next morning.

The fourth Japanese midget, on its way out of the harbor, attempted to torpedo the USS *St. Louis.* The light cruiser evaded the torpedoes and the small submarine disappeared.

The fifth midget sub vanished and was presumed lost to an American attack.

Before World War II, the United States and Japan believed their two navies would meet in the Pacific for a decisive fight. The Japanese thought a long-range submarine force could attack the American Fleet and reduce its numerical advantage. The ordinary submarine, however, traveled too slowly under water to catch fast surface ships. Imperial Navy torpedo technicians came up with a solution in the early 1930s: build small, high-speed midget submarines capable of intercepting and sinking a warship. Japanese planners realized they could use the little submarines—code named "Target A"—against ships at anchor in a harbor. The Imperial Japanese Navy had twenty midget subs in commission at the time of the attack on Pearl Harbor. Five midgets sank at Pearl Harbor on December 7, 1941, four in an attack on Sydney Harbor in May 1942, eight during the Guadalcanal campaign, and the remaining three off the Aleutian Islands, 1942–1943.

A Japanese memorial photograph (above) of the nine midget submariners lost at Pearl Harbor. Imperial Navy authorities erroneously gave the small subs credit for sinking the U.S. battleship *Arizona*, and the crews were lionized by the Japanese public. The Imperial Navy awarded them a posthumous promotion of two ranks—the equivalent of a medal of honor. Although nine submariners are shown in the photograph, there were actually ten. The missing man, Ensign Kazuo Sakamaki, was taken prisoner. This disgraced him in the eyes of the Japanese Navy and the memorial picture appeared without his image.

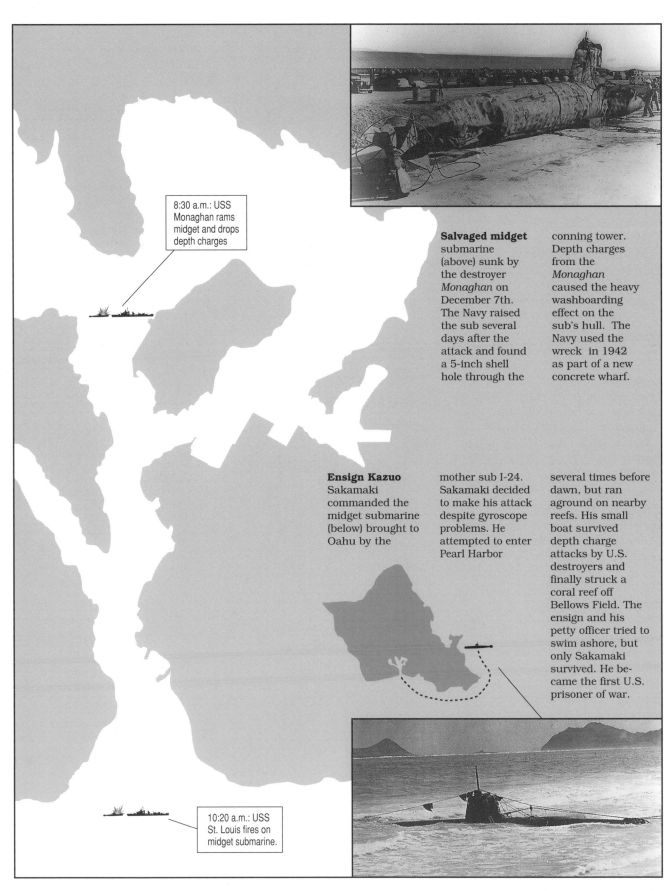

8:30 a.m.: USS Monaghan rams midget and drops depth charges

Salvaged midget submarine (above) sunk by the destroyer *Monaghan* on December 7th. The Navy raised the sub several days after the attack and found a 5-inch shell hole through the conning tower. Depth charges from the *Monaghan* caused the heavy washboarding effect on the sub's hull. The Navy used the wreck in 1942 as part of a new concrete wharf.

Ensign Kazuo Sakamaki commanded the midget submarine (below) brought to Oahu by the mother sub I-24. Sakamaki decided to make his attack despite gyroscope problems. He attempted to enter Pearl Harbor several times before dawn, but ran aground on nearby reefs. His small boat survived depth charge attacks by U.S. destroyers and finally struck a coral reef off Bellows Field. The ensign and his petty officer tried to swim ashore, but only Sakamaki survived. He became the first U.S. prisoner of war.

10:20 a.m.: USS St. Louis fires on midget submarine.

Second Wave

Shortly after takeoff from the carrier *Zuikaku* Lt. Commander Shigekazu Shimazaki, leader of the second air attack force, heard Fuchida's *"Tora, Tora, Tora"* message over his radio. He realized the first wave had achieved complete surprise at Pearl Harbor. The second wave was one hour behind the first and Shimazaki knew his 167 plane force would not have that advantage. Only after the raid did he find out that the first wave lost only nine aircraft: three fighters, one dive-bomber, and five torpedo planes.

The plan for the second assault called for the Kate high-level bombers and the Val dive-bombers to reverse roles. The Kates would bomb the airfields, while the more accurate Vals dive-bombed the warships at the harbor. No torpedo planes participated in this wave because their slow, low-altitude flight made them too good a target.

The Japanese saw huge columns of smoke rising over Pearl Harbor when they approached Oahu. At 8:54 a.m. Commander Shimazaki gave the order to attack.

Val dive-bomber (above) over Pearl Harbor.

As the second wave approached Oahu (left) its fighters, dive-bombers, and high-level bombers split up and went for their targets. The 80 dive-bombers headed for Pearl Harbor in four groups. The 54 Kate high-level bombers divided into three strike forces: 9 swung west to attack Ford Island, but missed the field in the intense black smoke; 18 Kates hit the hangars at Kaneohe; the remaining 27 blasted Hickam Field. The 35 Zero fighters broke into two sections: 17 approached Kaneohe where 9 strafed the hangar area, while the other 8 flew on to attack Bellows Field; the second group of 18 Zero fighters struck Ewa and Wheeler Fields.

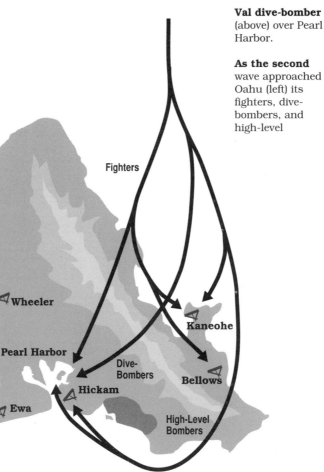

Fighters

◁ Wheeler

Kaneohe

Pearl Harbor

Dive-Bombers

Bellows ◁

◁ Hickam

◁ Ewa

High-Level Bombers

Second Attack Wave
8:54 AM

The second wave of Japanese raiders (above) meets fierce American anti-aircraft fire at Pearl Harbor. Many Japanese dive-bombers hit the cruisers and destroyers on the northwest side of Ford Island. The light cruiser *Raleigh*, already listing from a torpedo during the first wave, took a near miss, and a few seconds later, a direct hit aft. Just ahead of *Raleigh*, two more bombs missed the light cruiser *Detroit* by only 30 yards. Anti-aircraft fire from the sea-plane tender *Curtiss* attracted a dive-bomber a little after 9 a.m. The 550 pound bomb struck near the No. 1 crane and exploded below decks causing serious damage. At 9:30 a.m. a dive-bomber crashed about 500 yards off the destroyer *Montgomery's* port side. The Japanese pilot survived the crash and crawled out on the wing. When the *Montgomery* sent a boat to take him prisoner he pulled out a pistol, but was shot before he could use it. The second wave lost six Zero fighters and fourteen Val dive-bombers.

A dive-bomber (right) of the second wave after being hit by anti-aircraft fire. The Val crashed into the USS *Curtiss* seconds after this photo was taken.

Harbor Bombing—Second Wave

Seventy-eight Val dive-bombers led by Lt. Comdr. Takeshige Egusa attacked the ships in Pearl Harbor during the second wave. Finding Battleship Row covered with smoke, some of the Vals crossed the narrow channel to bomb the warships at the Navy Yard.

At 9:10 a.m. a near miss damaged the destroyer *Cummings* and the adjacent repair ship *Rigel*. One dock over, three bombs exploded near the cruiser *St. Louis*, but did little harm. About the same time another bomb crashed into the pier next to the USS *Honolulu* and holed the vessel's hull. Several bombs fell around the *Helena*, but the torpedoed cruiser escaped further damage.

Five hundred feet to the south, a bomb struck the battleship *Pennsylvania*—sister ship of the *Arizona*—killing fifteen men and wounding thirty-eight. In the floating dry dock, the destroyer *Shaw* took three direct hits which enveloped the ship in flames.

In spite of the destruction, many of the bombs missed their targets. The second attack wave damaged eight ships but sank only three.

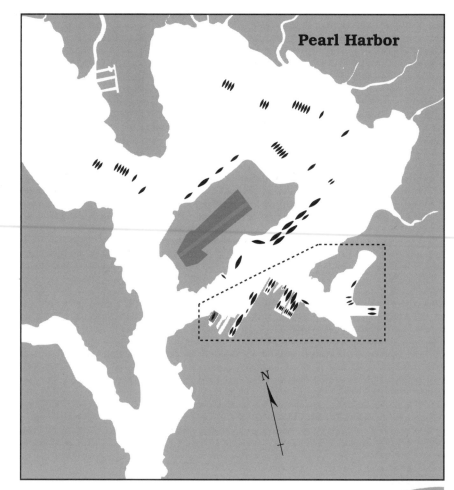

**Pearl Harbor Navy Yard
8:55 AM**

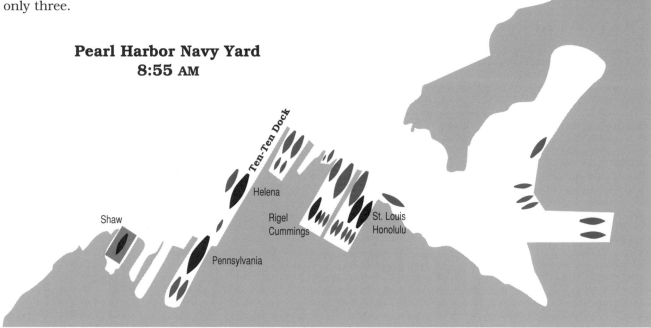

70

The view looking south down Battleship Row (left) late on Sunday morning, December 7th. In the foreground the USS *Arizona* lies sunk and burning. The flag, hoisted at 8 a.m. just as the attack began, is visible beside the aircraft crane on *Arizona's* fantail. That night two young ensigns returned to the *Arizona*, removed the colors and gave it to their superiors. It is believed cleanup crews burned the oil-soaked flag the following day.

A motor launch (left) rescues a sailor in the water near the burning USS *West Virginia*. The battleship suffered severe damage from at least seven torpedo hits and from oil fires that burned for twenty-four hours. *West Virginia's* captain, Mervyn Bennion, died on the bridge after being struck by shrapnel from a bomb explosion. He was awarded the Congressional Medal of Honor posthumously for his courage.

71

Sortie of the Nevada

One of the most dramatic moments of the attack occurred a few minutes before 9 a.m. when the battleship *Nevada* got underway. Although damaged by a torpedo in the first wave, *Nevada* managed (by having an extra boiler lit) to reach steam in forty-five minutes, instead of the normal two hours.

The battleship eased past the burning *Arizona* and headed for the harbor's entrance just as the Japanese second wave broke. Twenty-three *Kaga* dive-bombers spotted the moving ship and swept down to sink *Nevada* in the channel and block the harbor.

Numerous bombs exploded around the warship before the Japanese corrected their aim and scored five direct hits. These bombs ruptured the hull in two places and started many fires.

The battleship escaped the fate of the *Arizona*, however. The day before, *Nevada*'s crew replaced the warships' 14-inch shells as part of a normal ammunition rotation. They had not yet reloaded the required 2,800 bags of smokeless powder into the main magazines.

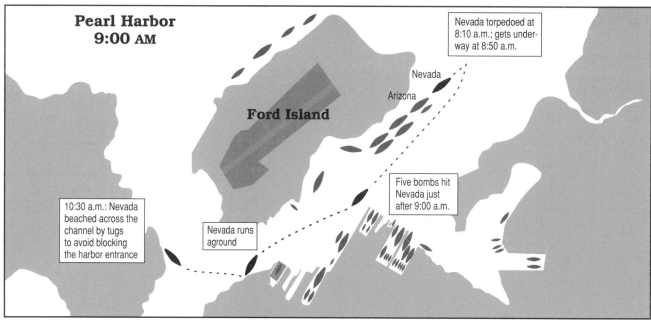

**Pearl Harbor
9:00 AM**

Ford Island

Nevada torpedoed at 8:10 a.m.; gets underway at 8:50 a.m.

Nevada

Arizona

Five bombs hit Nevada just after 9:00 a.m.

10:30 a.m.: Nevada beached across the channel by tugs to avoid blocking the harbor entrance

Nevada runs aground

Crewmen (left) survey *Nevada's* badly ruptured upper deck in front of Turret No.1. Most of the flooding resulted from the torpedo hole on the port side and two forward bomb hits. These explosions opened a triangular rip in *Nevada's* hull on the starboard side and a six foot hole on the port side. Fifty of *Nevada's* crew died during the attack. One hundred and nine more were wounded.

The *Nevada* (above) successfully beached on an even keel near Hospital Point to prevent sinking. The first officers to inspect *Nevada* after the attack were horrified. The front part of the ship was a mass of twisted steel and broken decks. Body parts littered the wreckage. The crew quickly overcame its shock and within a day cleared the debris, washed the decks, and prepared *Nevada* for salvage.

Cassin and Downes

At 9:10 a.m. just after the *Nevada* went aground across from Ford Island Naval Air Station, a squadron of dive-bombers from the carrier *Hiryu* attacked the Navy Yard. Their targets were the battleship *Pennsylvania* and the destroyers *Cassin* and *Downes*, which berthed together in Dry Dock No. 1

One bomb hit the *Pennsylvania's* boat deck, two struck the *Cassin*, and another destroyed the bridge of the *Downes*. Near misses cut off water and electric power to the dry dock. This and the thick black smoke made it impossible to fight the fires that engulfed the two smaller ships. Blazing fuel oil set off the destroyers' depth charges and torpedoes, and the *Cassin* rolled onto the *Downes*.

Four sailors ran onto the gangway just as the *Cassin* went over. Two of them made it to the dry dock; the other two were carried into the fiery wrecks.

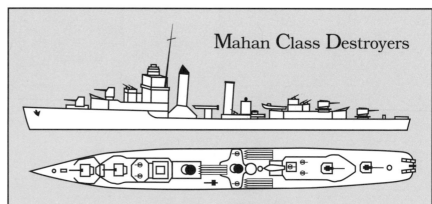

Mahan Class Destroyers

Destroyers were the workhorses of World War II. The most powerful small ships in the fleet, they were fast, maneuverable, and carried a strong torpedo armament. Because they displaced only 1,500 to 2,500 tons, these little ships could be built in great numbers. Although the United States Navy began World War II with 200 destroyers, 100 were obsolete World War I vintage "four stackers." The Navy built 18 destroyers of the modern Mahan class in 1934. Among them were the USS *Cassin* and the USS *Downes*. All of the Mahan class served in the Pacific during the war and six of the eighteen were lost in combat.

Length:	341 feet
Weight:	2,136 tons
Speed:	36 knots
Range:	6,500 miles at 12 knots
Guns:	Five 5-inch, four machine guns
Torpedoes:	Twelve 21-inch
Crew:	158

**Pearl Harbor Navy Yard
9:10 AM**

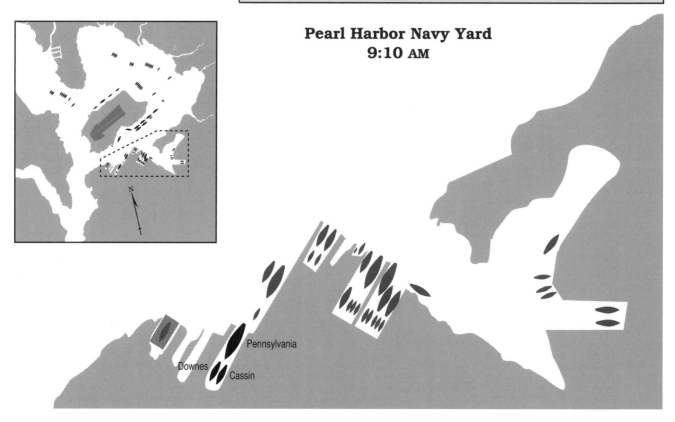

The USS *Cassin* collapsed against the USS *Downes* on December 8th. Battleship *Pennsylvania* sits behind the two destroyers. Smoke from the still burning *Arizona* rises in the background.

USS Shaw

A group of dive-bombers from the carrier *Akagi* veered off during the attack on the *Nevada* to look for fresh targets. They found the battleship *Pennsylvania* with destroyers, *Cassin* and *Downes* in Dry Dock No. 1, and the destroyer *Shaw* in floating Dry Dock No. 2 a few hundred yards west.

Three of the dive-bombers concentrated on the *Shaw*. Two 550 pound bombs penetrated the main deck near the 5-inch guns and exploded in the crew's mess on first platform deck. A third bomb passed through the bridge, ruptured the fuel tanks, and set the front half of the destroyer on fire.

This blaze eventually ignited the forward magazines, which detonated in an enormous ball of fire seen all over Pearl Harbor. A seaman at Ford Island Naval Air Station, almost half-a-mile away, had to dodge debris from the explosion. An Army major in Admiral Kimmel's office at Pacific Fleet Headquarters remembered the look of horror on the Admiral's face when the *Shaw* blew up.

The floating dry dock around the destroyer sank from the blast, and left the burning *Shaw* broken in two behind the bridge.

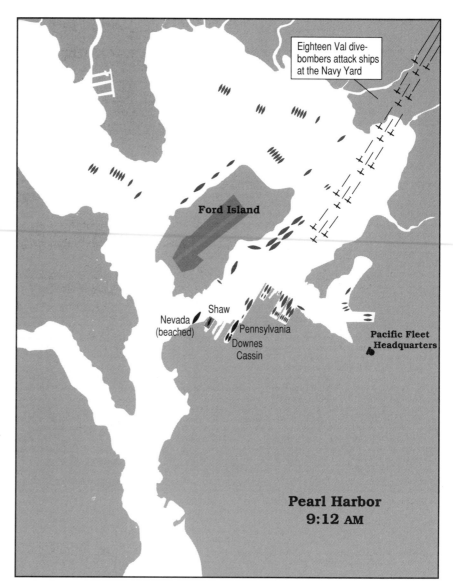

Eighteen Val dive-bombers attack ships at the Navy Yard

Ford Island

Nevada (beached)

Shaw

Pennsylvania

Downes

Cassin

Pacific Fleet Headquarters

Pearl Harbor 9:12 AM

USS *Shaw's* forward magazines explode (above) about 10 a.m. during the second attack wave. Undergoing repairs in dry dock, the Mahan class destroyer *Shaw* was an easy target for the squadron of dive-bombers led by Lt. Shohei Yamada.

After the attack (right) *Shaw* smoulders in the heavily damaged floating dry dock. The magazine explosion severed the ship's bow just behind the bridge. The aft part of the *Shaw* stayed afloat, and after inital repairs, became the foundation of the rebuilt destroyer.

Hickam Field—Second Wave

In the second wave, the Japanese committed 27 high-level Kate bombers to complete the destruction of Hickam Field. Heavy anti-aircraft fire met the attackers, and several groups of high-level bombers flying in a V-formation were forced to make additional runs over the field to hit their targets.

The bombs destroyed an aircraft repair facility and the power cable to the engineering shops. They damaged the steam plant, main shop, armament and equipment buildings. Hangars 13 and 15 took direct hits, and several 500 pound bombs cratered the baseball diamond, which the Japanese erroneously believed to be the site of an underground fuel supply. One of these explosions killed two airmen who had set up a machine gun on the baseball field.

While the bombs exploded, ground crews at Hickam struggled desperately to load their few undamaged planes with bombs. Eighteen Zero fighters from the carriers *Akagi* and *Kaga* strafed the field to prevent this counter-attack. A sergeant and an airman, running from the flight line, hit the dirt just as a Zero made its pass. When the sergeant raised his head, he saw that the machine-gun bullets had cut his fellow soldier in two.

The intensity of the attack on Hickam Field is reflected by the ratio of Hickam losses to total Army Air Force casualties on Oahu. Army Air Force figures after the attack were 163 killed, 336 wounded, and 43 missing. Hickam's losses were 121 killed (75%), 274 wounded (81%), and 37 missing (86%).

The Japanese destroyed a total of four B-17s, twelve B-18s, and two A-20 bombers at Hickam—a little over 30% of the Field's total strength.

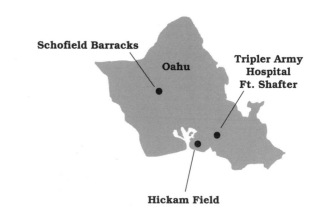

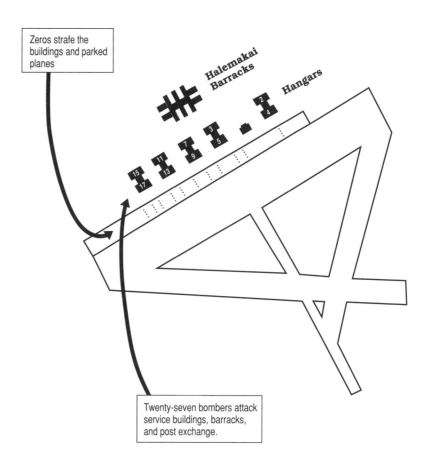

Zeros strafe the buildings and parked planes

Twenty-seven bombers attack service buildings, barracks, and post exchange.

Hickam Field
9:05 AM

American airmen (left) killed during the strafing of Hickam Field. Even before the attack ended, Hawaii's well-organized disaster services began to provide emergency medical care for hundreds of wounded men. By 9:20 a.m., forty-five ambulances rushed to Hickam. At Tripler Army Hospital, badly wounded patients arrived until late afternoon. Medics brought in so many injured that blood covered the stairways at the hospital entrance. In response to the Army's request, civilian doctors and nurses volunteered their services. Airmen killed at Hickam Field were buried in the Army's permanent cemetery at Schofield Barracks.

Capt. Raymond Swenson's B-17 (below) lies burned-out and broken near Hangar No. 5 following the Hickam attack. This bomber was part of the group that arrived from the mainland during the first wave. Japanese cannon shells set off magnesium flares which destroyed the rear half of the aircraft.

Capt. Roland Boyer and Private Lawrence Haslett (right) survey the bomb damage to Hangar 11. A Japanese Zero fighter swooped down with machine guns and cannon firing while this photograph was taken. The two men and the Signal Corps photographer ran for cover and escaped injury.

Wheeler Field/Kaneohe Air Station—Second Wave

Wheeler Field

Twenty-five Val dive-bombers from the aircraft carrier *Zuikaku* bombed and strafed Wheeler Field in the first wave. In the second attack the Japanese planned to strafe Wheeler and pin down U.S. fighters with Zeros from *Kaga* and *Soryu*.

The first group of eight *Kaga* Zeros machine-gunned Wheeler then flew on to attack Hickam Field. The second group of Zeros hit Kaneohe Naval Air Station and then flew toward Wheeler. They never made it. Six U.S. P-36 fighters from Wheeler Field jumped them on the way. These were one of three small groups of American interceptors to become airborne during the raid. They broke up this approaching attack on Wheeler Field and claimed a total of eleven enemy planes shot down. The Japanese destroyed or damaged 83 of Wheeler's 153 aircraft and killed 37 Americans.

Remains of Wheeler's tent barracks (above) after a fire caused by Japanese dive-bombers in the first wave. Located between Hangars No. 6 and No. 7 in a former recreation field, Tent City was full of sleeping airmen when the attack began.

Wreckage of Hangar No. 1 (below). This bombed-out hangar, part of Wheeler's Base Engineering complex, housed the sheet metal, electrical, fabric, machine, and carpenter shops. The first bomb to drop on Wheeler Field struck this building.

**Wheeler Field
9:10 AM**

Eight Japanese Zeros strafe U.S. fighters while they taxi to the runway

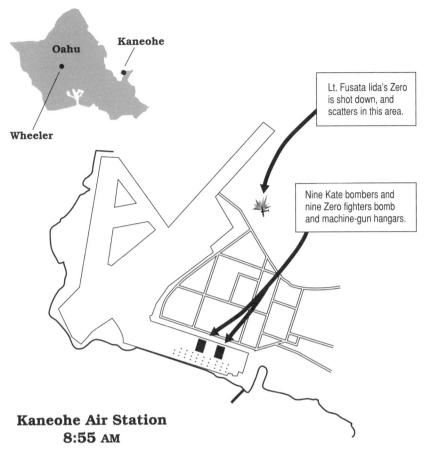

Kaneohe Air Station
8:55 AM

Lt. Fusata Iida's Zero is shot down, and scatters in this area.

Nine Kate bombers and nine Zero fighters bomb and machine-gun hangars.

Kaneohe Naval Air Station

The Japanese returned to Kaneohe with high-level bombers to finish what their strafing Zeros had begun in the first wave. Eighteen Kates bombed the hangars from 6,500 ft. altitude. This attack set fire to Hangar No. 1, damaged Hangar No. 3 and destroyed four more PBY seaplanes. Eight *Hiryu* Zeros strafed the air station, then flew southeast to shoot up Bellows Field.

After their departure, nine Zeros from *Soryu* attacked Kaneohe. While they made their runs, U.S. machine gun fire hit Lt. Fusata Iida's Zero and holed its gas tank. Iida realized he could not return to the carriers, and firing his guns, dived on the Kaneohe Armory. He flew into the automatic rifle fire of an ordnanceman named Sands. This duel of sailor vs. Zero continued until Lt. Iida passed over Sands and crashed into a nearby hill.

Ewa Air Station/Bellows Field—Second Wave

Ewa Air Station

Ewa Marine Corps Air Station started the morning of December 7th with forty-eight aircraft of various types. In the first wave, strafing Japanese Zero fighters destroyed many of the station's planes. Ewa had the misfortune to be the rendezvous point for the raiders when they finished their assignments; it became the place to expend any remaining ammunition.

Just after a group of Val dive-bombers hit the field at 8:30 a.m., six U.S. Navy planes from the aircraft carrier *Enterprise* made an emergency landing. Ewa's commander, Lieutenant Colonel Claude Larkin, immediately ordered them back into the air until the attack was over.

In the lull between the first and second waves, marines scrambled to the wrecked planes and salvaged guns to set up anti-aircraft batteries. When a group of Zero fighters returned to strafe the surviving aircraft on Ewa's runway, the Americans put up a curtain of heavy machine-gun fire. Nevertheless, by 10 a.m. the Japanese had seriously damaged or destroyed thirty-three planes at Ewa Field.

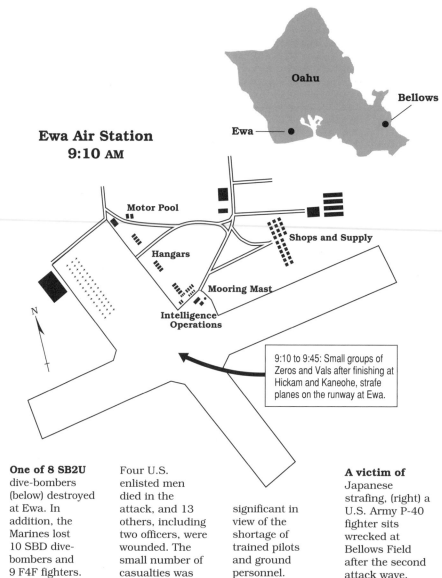

Ewa Air Station 9:10 AM

Oahu

Bellows

Ewa

Motor Pool

Shops and Supply

Hangars

Mooring Mast

Intelligence Operations

N

9:10 to 9:45: Small groups of Zeros and Vals after finishing at Hickam and Kaneohe, strafe planes on the runway at Ewa.

One of 8 SB2U dive-bombers (below) destroyed at Ewa. In addition, the Marines lost 10 SBD dive-bombers and 9 F4F fighters.

Four U.S. enlisted men died in the attack, and 13 others, including two officers, were wounded. The small number of casualties was significant in view of the shortage of trained pilots and ground personnel.

A victim of Japanese strafing, (right) a U.S. Army P-40 fighter sits wrecked at Bellows Field after the second attack wave.

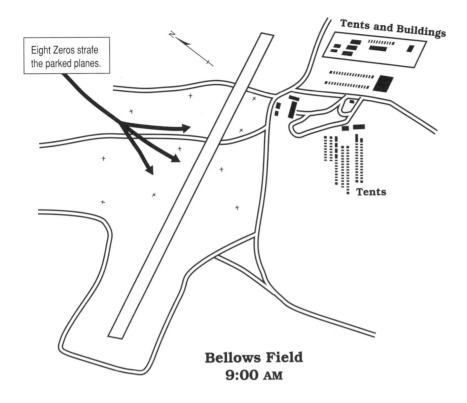

Eight Zeros strafe the parked planes.

Tents and Buildings

Tents

**Bellows Field
9:00 AM**

Bellows Field

The first attack spared Bellows the destruction inflicted on other air fields around Oahu. This respite allowed ground crews time to disperse the twelve P-40s and nine O-47s from their single file anti-sabotage positions.

Unfortunately, as part of normal maintenance practice, airmen removed the machine guns on the P-40s for routine cleaning the previous night. Reinstalling, reloading, and calibrating the guns was a time consuming process. When eight *Hiryu* Zeros of the second wave attacked Bellows, ordnance crews had only finished three planes.

Lt. George Whiteman's P-40 attempted to take off, but a Zero shot him down in flames. Lt. Hans Christianson fell to machine gun fire getting into his plane, and Lt. Sam Bishop made it into the air, but was quickly downed.

Final Action

Morning:

The light cruiser USS *St. Louis* was docked at the Pearl Harbor Navy Yard for boiler repairs when the attack began. Through frantic efforts, the ship reached steam power at 9:30 a.m. and backed out of its mooring.

Captain George Rood took the *St. Louis* south, down the straight channel at full speed toward the sea. Near Pearl Harbor's mouth, lookouts sighted two torpedoes coming in from the starboard at a 45° angle. Unable to maneuver in the narrow passage, the captain and his crew braced for the explosion. Miraculously, the torpedoes hit a coral outcrop near Buoy No. 1 and exploded before reaching the ship.

The *St. Louis* spotted a midget sub's conning tower 1,000 yards away and fired several 5-inch salvos at the target. The battle of Pearl Harbor ended the way it had begun—with an American warship attacking a Japanese midget submarine.

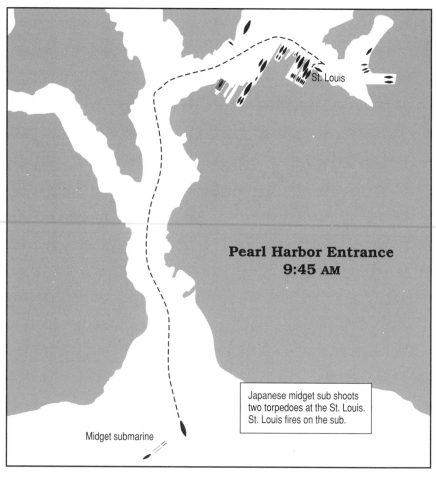

**Pearl Harbor Entrance
9:45 AM**

St. Louis

Midget submarine

Japanese midget sub shoots two torpedoes at the St. Louis. St. Louis fires on the sub.

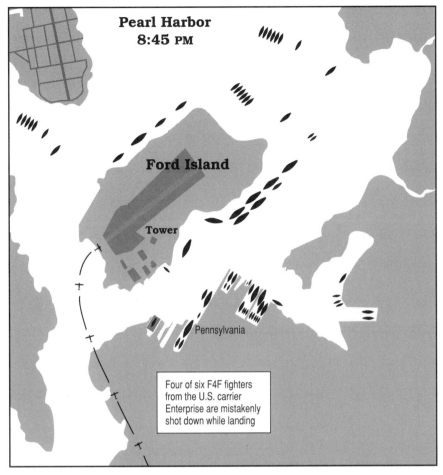

Pearl Harbor
8:45 PM

Ford Island

Tower

Pennsylvania

Four of six F4F fighters
from the U.S. carrier
Enterprise are mistakenly
shot down while landing

Evening:

After the attack, American naval units conducted a confused and fruitless search for the Japanese Task force. On Oahu, in the hours that followed, conflicting signals and a general trigger-happiness caused several tragedies.

The carrier *Enterprise* began a sweep for the enemy, believed to be retreating south to the Marshall Islands. *Enterprise* launched eighteen torpedo bombers, four scout bombers, and six F4F fighters. Finding no Japanese, all planes but the fighters returned to the carrier. The F4Fs flew on to land at Oahu.

The control tower on Ford Island advised all ships in the harbor of approaching American planes, and ordered the fighters to come in. But fear overrode orders, and the *Pennsylvania* fired at the landing fighters. The entire harbor began shooting and downed four of the F4Fs, killing three American pilots.

Light cruiser
St. Louis (left) on its way out of the harbor passes the sinking battleship *California.*

Soldiers (right) dig in and await the next Japanese attack. The night of December 7th found everyone on Oahu braced for invasion. At Hickam and Wheeler fields hundreds of airmen abandoned their damaged barracks to sleep in the open. Stray machine gun fire around the harbor killed one *Utah* survivor and wounded another.

Honolulu Casualties

Eight miles from Pearl Harbor, Honolulu began Sunday, December 7th quietly. Even the sound of bombs and columns of smoke from Pearl Harbor failed to alarm many Honolulu residents who were used to constant military training exercises.

The outbreak of war became apparent at 8:05 a.m. when the first of forty explosions racked the city. Ironically, the Japanese refrained from directly bombing Honolulu; improperly fused American anti-aircraft shells from Pearl Harbor created the unintended artillery bombardment.

Alarmed citizens called the fire department, but most of their equipment was at Hickam Field, battling fires. After conferring by phone with President Roosevelt, Territorial Governor Joseph E. Poindexter declared a state of emergency and put Hawaii under martial law. Authorities later determined 68 civilians had been killed and 35 wounded.

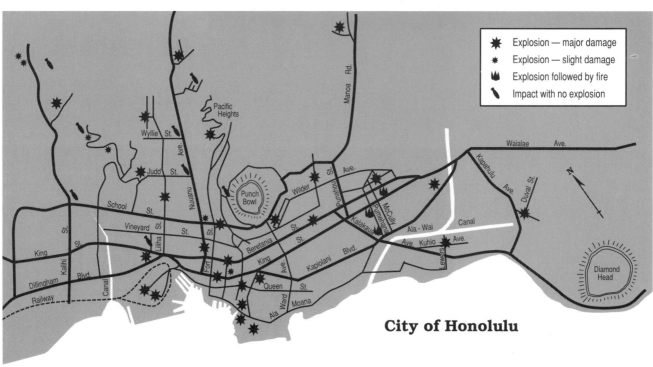

City of Honolulu

86

Honolulu building (left) blown up by an errant U.S. anti-aircraft blast. Shells destroyed or damaged structures all over the city. Several explosions caused a severe fire on McCully Street. Another shell started a blaze at Lunalilo School on Pumehana Street. Civilian medical personnel set up a first-aid clinic on the school grounds while residents fought the fire. Four Navy Yard workers, returning to Pearl Harbor, died when a shell landed near their car on Judd Street.

Normally published only Monday through Saturday, the *Honolulu Star-Bulletin* rushed out three extras on December 7th to meet the demand for information. Local radio stations KGMB and KGU interrupted their morning programs to call all Army, Navy, and Marine personnel back to duty. Further calls notified doctors and nurses to report to their clinics for emergency service. Despite shock at the attack, Oahu experienced little panic. Civil defense, aided by hundreds of volunteers, quickly went into action.

Honolulu Star-Bulletin— 1st Extra

Oahu was attacked at 7:55 this morning by Japanese planes. The rising sun, emblem of Japan, was seen on plane wing tips. Wave after wave of bombers streamed through the clouded morning sky from the southwest and flung their missiles on a city resting in peaceful Sabbath calm.

Within 10 minutes the city was in an uproar. As bombs fell on many parts of the city, and in defense areas, the defenders of the islands went into quick action.

Army intelligence officers at Fort Shafter announced shortly after 9 a.m. the fact of the bombardment by an enemy. . . . Civilians are ordered to stay off the streets until further notice.

87

Declaration of War

News of the Pearl Harbor attack stunned the country and indelibly marked the day in memory for each American. At 1:40 in the afternoon, Washington time, Secretary of the Navy Frank Knox called the White House and informed President Roosevelt that Pearl Harbor was under attack. The President's visiting friend and close personal advisor, Harry Hopkins, is reported to have said. "That can't be true. They must mean the Philippines."

While the disastrous news poured in, Roosevelt coordinated defense moves with Army Chief of Staff General George C. Marshall. Late in the afternoon the president dictated the first draft of his message to Congress, asking for a declaration of war against Japan. At 8:30 p.m. he briefed the cabinet and read them his draft, and then met with the leaders of Congress until midnight.

With the news of the Japanese treachery, a tremendous wave of shock, outrage, and anger swept over the United States. This "sneak attack" during the long-running peace negotiations infuriated the people. That Sunday, Americans united in the determination to utterly defeat Japan.

The next day at 12:20 p.m. a convoy of ten black limousines arrived on the Capitol grounds. The cars parked at the south entrance and the presidential party entered the House chamber. The entire Senate filed in, and then the Supreme Court. At 12:29 President Roosevelt went to the rostrum. After a resounding ovation he began his address to Congress: "Yesterday, December 7, 1941—a date which will live in infamy—the United States of America was suddenly and deliberately attacked by naval and air forces of the Empire of Japan. . . ."

Franklin Delano Roosevelt
Thirty-second President of the United States

Franklin D. Roosevelt (FDR) was born into a wealthy upstate New York family on January 30, 1882. Educated by private tutors and at the Groton School, Roosevelt entered Harvard in 1900. At the university he met a distant cousin, Anna Eleanor Roosevelt, whom he married in 1905. Upon graduation from Columbia Law School, Franklin Roosevelt's interests turned to politics, and in 1910 he was elected as a Democrat to the New York State Senate. In appreciation for his support in the 1912 presidential election, Woodrow Wilson appointed him assistant secretary of the Navy. Roosevelt gained a national reputation in this office, and in 1920 the Democrats nominated him for vice-president on the ticket with James Cox. That bid lost to a Republican landslide. One year later, Roosevelt contracted polio and suffered paralysis in his legs. He remained active in Democratic politics, however, and in 1928 won the governorship of New York. The 1929 stock market crash and the arrival of the Great Depression rapidly transformed national politics. In 1932 Roosevelt became president of the United States in an electoral landslide, after promising a "New Deal" for the American people. He was re-elected in 1936, 1940, and 1944—an unprecedented four terms. In the face of strong American isolationism, FDR gradually evolved a policy to support the democracies in Europe. When war broke out in 1939, he arranged massive Lend-Lease aid to Britian in its struggle against Nazi Germany. His administration tried by peaceful means to halt Japanese aggression in East Asia. After the Pearl Harbor attack he led the nation in its successful prosecution of the war. He died on April 12, 1945 at Warm Springs, Georgia, four months before the end of the Second World War.

U.S. Declaration of War

Yesterday, December 7, 1941—a date which will live in infamy—the United States of America was suddenly and deliberately attacked by naval and air forces of the Empire of Japan.

The United States was at peace with that Nation and, at the solicitation of Japan, was still in conversation with its Government and its Emperor, looking toward the maintenance of peace in the Pacific. Indeed, one hour after Japanese squadrons had commenced bombing in Oahu, the Japanese Ambassador to the United States and his colleague delivered to the Secretary of State a formal reply to a recent American message. While this reply stated that it seemed useless to continue the existing diplomatic negotiations, it contained no threat or hint of war or armed attack.

It will be recorded that the distance of Hawaii from Japan makes it obvious that the attack was deliberately planned many days or even weeks ago. During the intervening time the Japanese Government has deliberately sought to deceive the United States by false statements and expressions of hope for continued peace.

The attack yesterday on the Hawaiian Islands has caused severe damage to American naval and military forces. Very many American lives have been lost. In addition, American ships have been reported torpedoed on the high seas between San Francisco and Honolulu.

Yesterday the Japanese Government also launched an attack against Malaya. Last night Japanese forces attacked Hong Kong. Last night Japanese forces attacked Guam. Last night Japanese forces attacked the Philippine Islands. Last night the Japanese attacked Wake Island. This morning the Japanese attacked Midway Island.

Japan has, therefore, undertaken a surprise offensive extending throughout the Pacific area. The facts of yesterday speak for themselves. The people of the United States have already formed their opinions, and well understand the implications to the very life and safety of our Nation.

As Commander-in-Chief of the Army and Navy I have directed all measures be taken for our defense. Always will we remember the character of the onslaught against us. No matter how long it may take us to overcome this premeditated invasion, the American people in their righteous might will win through to absolute victory.

I believe I interpret the will of the Congress and of the people when I assert that we will not only defend ourselves to the uttermost but will make very certain that this form of treachery shall never endanger us again. Hostilities exist. There is no blinking at the fact that our people, our territory, and our interest are in grave danger.

With confidence in our armed forces, with the unbounded determination of our people, we will gain the inevitable triumph, so help us God.

I ask that the Congress declare that since the unprovoked and dastardly attack by Japan on Sunday, December 7th, a state of war has existed between the United States and the Japanese Empire.

U.S. Losses

Two hours after it began, the Japanese attack on Pearl Harbor was over. Although Commander Fuchida urged another strike on the Americans, the cautious Admiral Nagumo turned the First Air Fleet back to Japan.

At Pearl Harbor, columns of dense black smoke from the burning ships drifted south on the morning breeze. Five of the eight U.S. battleships in the harbor were sunk, the other three lightly damaged. Further casualties included three light cruisers, three destroyers, and four auxiliary ships. Altogether 18 out of the 96 vessels at Pearl Harbor were either sunk or seriously damaged.

The naval and marine air stations at Ford Island, Kaneohe, and Ewa lost 87 planes and had 31 damaged. The Army Air Force lost a total of 74 aircraft at Hickam, Wheeler, and Bellows fields; 128 planes sustained damage. More grievously, 2,388 Americans were killed, missing, or subsequently died from their wounds. Another 1,178 were wounded, but recovered.

In spite of their military success, the Japanese failed to fire a single bullet into the 4,500,000 barrels of oil stockpiled in tanks around the harbor. This oil powered the U.S. Pacific Fleet in 1942 on Lt. Col. James Doolittle's Tokyo raid, and at the battles of the Coral Sea and Midway. The Japanese also left the ship repair facilities of Pearl Harbor intact, a decision they came to regret.

Ironically, the survival of all U.S. aircraft carriers, and the loss of the battleships, forced the Navy to reconstitute the Pacific Fleet into carrier task forces—a naval strategy that won the war.

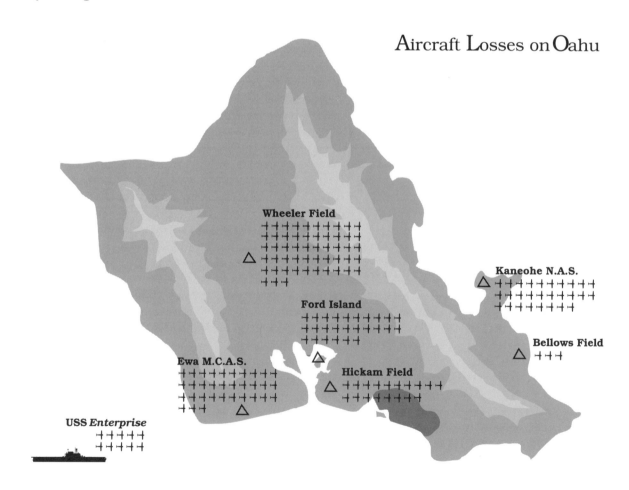

Aircraft Losses on Oahu

Based on figures from the U.S. Congress, Joint Committee on the Investigation of the Pearl Harbor Attack

90

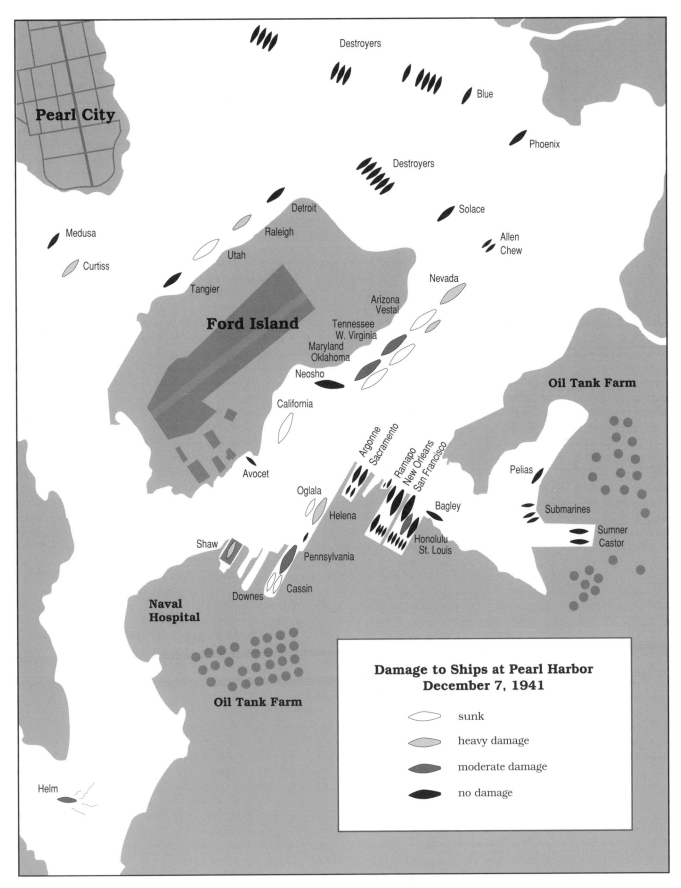

Pearl City

Destroyers

Blue

Phoenix

Destroyers

Solace

Allen
Chew

Medusa

Curtiss

Detroit

Raleigh

Utah

Nevada

Tangier

Arizona
Vestal

Ford Island

Tennessee
W. Virginia

Maryland
Oklahoma

Neosho

Oil Tank Farm

California

Avocet

Argonne
Sacramento

Ramapo
New Orleans
San Francisco

Pelias

Oglala

Bagley

Submarines

Helena

Honolulu
St. Louis

Sumner
Castor

Shaw

Pennsylvania

**Naval
Hospital**

Downes

Cassin

Oil Tank Farm

Damage to Ships at Pearl Harbor
December 7, 1941

     sunk

     heavy damage

     moderate damage

     no damage

Helm

Salvage

Capt. Homer N. Wallin assumed command of the Pearl Harbor Salvage Organization on Jan. 9, 1942 and began one of the most historic chapters in the annals of warship salvage. Headquartered at the Pearl Harbor Navy Yard, his organization managed hundreds of divers and engineers in the systematic repair of almost all the damaged ships.

Wallin's men directed one of their first efforts to the shattered USS *Arizona*. Divers surveyed the wreck and found the aft portion of the battleship relatively intact, but the forward half virtually destroyed. They salvaged the six 14-inch guns in the two aft turrets, and removed the above-water superstructure for scrap. In 1962, the United States dedicated a permanent memorial over the ship.

USS Arizona

USS Nevada

Nevada was beached near the harbor entrance on Dec. 7th to prevent sinking. Close inspection after the attack revealed a torpedo hole in the bow and five bomb hits on the upper deck and superstructure. Two 550 pound bombs struck the forecastle. A third hit in front of Turret No. 1 and blew a large hole in the upper and main decks. A fourth bomb glanced off the foremast and detonated at the base of the smokestack. The fifth exploded near the galley.

Salvage work on *Nevada* began immediately. Navy crews patched the bomb holes and pumped out the water. On May 1, 1942, after temporary repairs, the battleship sailed to Puget Sound Navy Yard. Seven months later, thoroughly modernized, *Nevada* rejoined the Pacific Fleet.

USS Oklahoma

Five torpedoes struck the *Oklahoma* within seven minutes. The battleship quickly capsized, rotating 150 degrees before coming to rest on the solid bottom of Pearl Harbor. The turrets, masts, and superstructure were completely submerged in the mud.

After careful surveys in 1942 the Navy decided to float and drydock the 29,000 ton warship. On March 8, 1943, twenty-one electric winches, anchored into Ford Island, began to right the capsized vessel. Salvage crews found torpedo holes all along the *Oklahoma's* port side. The Navy considered the ship too damaged to rebuild, and decommissioned it in Sept. 1944. Sold for scrap in 1946, *Oklahoma* sank during a storm five hundred miles northeast of Hawaii while being towed back to the United States.

USS West Virginia

West Virginia's salvage turned out to be a difficult job for Captain Wallin's group. The ship sat, decks awash, in Battleship Row with seven torpedo hits in its hull. Four torpedoes struck on or below the armor belt and opened the ship's port side to the sea. Two more hit the battleship while it listed, then detonated on the second armored deck. The last torpedo knocked off the rudder.

Using tremendous underwater concrete patches, the engineers raised *West Virginia* on May 17, 1942. After temporary repairs, the battleship sailed under its own power to Puget Sound Navy Yard to be completely modernized. *West Virginia* rejoined the Fleet in 1944, fought its way across the Pacific, and saw the Japanese surrender in Tokyo Bay on September 2, 1945.

Salvage

USS California

Two torpedoes and one bomb struck USS *California* on December 7th. A number of manholes and ventilation ducts were open for a planned inspection the next morning, and this caused the battleship's progressive flooding and ultimate sinking three days later. *California* came to rest on the bottom with a list of five degrees to port.

Pearl Harbor's salvage team first removed the guns and other parts of the superstructure. Divers closed small openings in the ship and plugged the torpedo holes with large wooden patches. *California* reached dry dock on April 9, 1942. Six months later the ship sailed for Puget Sound Navy Yard. Completely rebuilt by Sept. 1943, the modernized warship fought in the Marianas and the Philippines.

USS Pennsylvania

On the morning of the attack USS *Pennsylvania* was in Dry Dock No. 1 for routine alignment of its propellers and shafts. During the second wave, a 550 pound bomb crashed into the battleship's boat deck, damaged the five-inch guns, and exploded two decks below. The blast killed fifteen men and wounded another thirty-eight.

The Navy Yard quickly repaired *Pennsylvania*, and the ship returned to service on December 20th. Modernized in late 1942, *Pennsylvania* fought with the Pacific Fleet in the Marshall Islands and the Philippines. In 1945, off Okinawa, a torpedo struck the *Pennsylvania*. Seriously damaged, the battleship finished the war after temporary repairs. The Navy scuttled the obsolete *Pennsylvania* in 1948.

USS Maryland

USS *Maryland* lay inboard of *Oklahoma*, and like the *Tennessee* escaped torpedo attack. Two bombs struck the *Maryland*, but were duds. The first ripped through the forecastle awning and damaged some of the compartments below. The second hit the bow, tore a small hole in the hull, and caused considerable flooding.

Salvage crews from the Navy Yard built a caisson around the hole in the bow and made temporary repairs. The ship returned to active duty on December 20th. *Maryland* spent 1942 and part of 1943 in the southwest Pacific on patrol. Late in 1943 the battleship took part in the bombardment of Tarawa. The ship was overhauled the following year, and went on to fight in the invasion of the Marianas and in the Philippines.

USS Tennessee

Moored inboard of the battleship *West Virginia*, the *Tennessee* escaped torpedo attack, but was wedged against the forward quay by the sinking *West Virginia*. Burning oil from the *Arizona*, two hundred feet away, engulfed *Tennessee*'s stern. Two large bombs struck the warship but failed to explode. Their impacts damaged Turrets No. 2 and 3.

To free the vessel, the Navy Yard dynamited the forward quay on December 16th. Four days later, after temporary repairs, the battleship returned to service. Puget Sound Navy Yard overhauled *Tennessee* the next year, and the warship rejoined the Pacific Fleet. *Tennessee* was damaged by coastal artillery during the 1944 invasion of Saipan, and again in 1945 when a kamikaze struck the ship.

Salvage

USS Utah

Three torpedoes hit USS *Utah* on the port side during the initial attack on Ford Island's cruiser line. The target ship quickly flooded and capsized with a loss of fifty-eight sailors.

After successfully raising the battleship *Oklahoma* in 1943, Pearl Harbor's salvage group repeated the technique with the *Utah.* A series of powerful electric winches on Ford Island righted the *Utah* to an angle of 38 degrees before the Navy decided, for economic reasons, to forgo further salvage.

In 1972, the government established the USS Utah Memorial to commemorate the loss of the ship and crew. Each morning a Naval color guard raises the flag at a simple concrete platform on the northwest shore of Ford Island to honor the USS *Utah.*

USS Raleigh

Moored in a berth normally used by an aircraft carrier, the USS *Raleigh* took a torpedo hit in the opening minutes of the attack. The sixteen-year-old warship listed to port. At 9 a.m. a dive-bomber hit the light cruiser with a 550 pound bomb. The crew jettisoned all removable top weight and counterflooded the ship to prevent capsizing.

After a temporary patch to the hull, *Raleigh* entered Dry Dock No. 1 on January 3, 1942. There, the Navy Yard repaired the ship's bomb damage and torpedo hole. In late February 1942, *Raleigh* sailed to Mare Island Navy Yard for a complete refit of the engine and electrical systems, and for modernization. The overhauled cruiser returned to service in the Pacific and fought in the Aleutian campaign.

USS Curtiss

Located west of Ford Island, the seaplane tender *Curtiss* opened fire with its anti-aircaft guns when the raid began. Half an hour later, at 8:30 a.m., the ship spotted a midget sub and hit the intruder twice with its 5-inch guns.

During the second attack wave, a Val dive-bomber crashed into *Curtiss'* forward crane and burned on the boat deck. The crew was fighting the blaze when four Vals bombed the ship, scoring one hit and three near misses. The bomb passed through three levels, detonated on the main deck, and started several fires. This explosion caused widespread shrapnel damage to wires, piping, and steam lines. The Navy Yard made temporary repairs in December, and finished refitting *Curtiss* when spare parts arrived in May 1942.

USS Helena

The new light cruiser USS *Helena* was tied up along the Ten-Ten Dock on December 7th. At 7:57 a.m. a torpedo passed under the adjacent *Oglala* and hit *Helena* on the starboard side. The No. 1 engine room and a nearby boiler room flooded.

On December 10th, *Helena* entered Dry Dock No. 2 for temporary repairs. Three weeks later, the cruiser sailed to Mare Island Navy Yard in California for overhaul. *Helena* rejoined the Pacific Fleet in the summer of 1942 and took part in the savage battles off Guadalcanal. The ship's luck ran out on July 6, 1943 at the Battle of Kula Gulf in the Solomon Islands. Three Japanese long lance torpedoes struck the *Helena* in a night action and the light cruiser jack-knifed and sank.

Salvage

USS Oglala

Oglala, an old mine-layer, was moored outboard of the light cruiser *Helena* at the Ten-Ten Dock on December 7th. A torpedo passed under *Oglala* and exploded against *Helena*. The pressure wave shattered *Oglala's* plating on the port side, and the ship slowly capsized. Considered a total loss at first, the Navy Yard decided to salvage *Oglala* rather than scrap the ship and risk damaging the Ten-Ten Dock.

Divers attached ten large pontoons to the ship, and injected compressed air into the hull. Once afloat, in April 1942, the Navy Yard patched *Oglala's* plating. After temporary repairs in dry dock, the mine-layer sailed to California for a complete overhaul. In February 1944, *Oglala*, now a repair ship, rejoined the Pacific Fleet.

USS Shaw

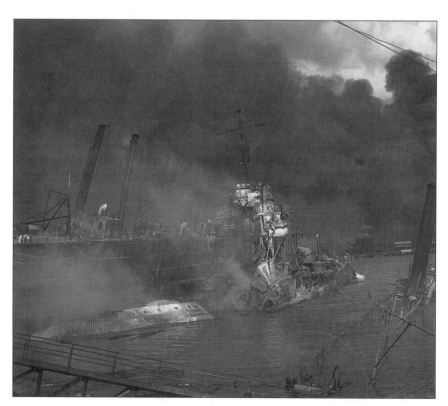

When salvage crews surveyed the wreckage of the USS *Shaw*, few believed the destroyer would ever sail again. Three Japanese bomb hits and the resulting forward magazine explosion cut the ship in two. Fortunately, the rear half of the destroyer stayed afloat in relatively good condition.

The Navy Yard decided to recover the *Shaw*. They attached a temporary bow and bridge house to the rear part of the ship. After a few sea trials, the *Shaw* sailed under its own power to Mare Island Navy Yard in California for a complete reconstruction. In the fall of 1942 the ship joined the Pacific Fleet as a first-line destroyer. *Shaw* fought in the battles of the Santa Cruz Islands, Guadalcanal, and Leyte Gulf in the Philippines, and won eleven battle stars.

USS Cassin

Japanese dive-bombers attacked the *Cassin* at 8:50 a.m on December 7th. One bomb crashed through the destroyer's hull and exploded on the floor of the dry dock. Fragments pierced the fuel tanks and started a severe fire. Another bomb hit *Cassin* amidships while the crew abandoned the burning destroyer. At 9:15 the Navy Yard flooded the dry dock to fight the fires. *Cassin* came afloat, became unstable, and fell over onto the adjacent *Downes*. Salvage crews found the toppled destroyer pocked with holes, and its keel warped.

The Navy Yard stripped out *Cassin's* machinery and sent it to Mare Island to be fitted into a new hull. The rebuilt USS *Cassin* rejoined the fleet in 1943, and took part in the Philippines and Marianas campaigns.

USS Downes

Downes sat adjacent to *Cassin* in Dry Dock No. 1 when a bomb passed through *Cassin* and exploded in the dry dock between the two ships. Shrapnel pierced both destroyers' exposed fuel tanks and started oil fires. These conflagrations eventually reached the *Downes'* torpedoes and the forward powder magazine, and set off secondary explosions. A torpedo blew up near the *Downes'* stack and ripped a large hole in the deck and side of the ship.

Salvage crews found the hull twisted, and the ship riddled with holes. They removed the destroyer's machinery and sent it to Mare Island to be fitted into a new hull. The recommissioned *Downes* returned to the Pacific Fleet in 1943, and served in the campaigns of Saipan and the Philippines.

Fate of the Commanders

Admiral Husband E. Kimmel

The searing American defeat at Pearl Harbor immediately raised questions of responsibility. Admiral Kimmel had the misfortune to be the obvious scapegoat. The Navy relieved Kimmel of his command on December 16th. He stayed in Hawaii until the Roberts Commission, the first of eight investigations on the Pearl Harbor attack, finished its work in January 1942. Kimmel retired in February 1942 under pressure from the government. Although threatened with a court-martial, it never materialized, and the Admiral spent the rest of his life defending his conduct. He died in May 1968 at the age of 86.

Lt. General Walter C. Short

The U.S. Army relieved General Short on December 16, 1941. He testified before the Roberts Commission on Oahu in late December, and left Hawaii for San Francisco in early January 1942. Two weeks later, the Roberts Commission released its edited conclusion to the press that Short and Kimmel were guilty of "dereliction of duty." General Short retired in March 1942, and subsequently worked for the Ford Motor Company as manager of a defense plant. He died in Dallas on September 3, 1949 and was buried with full military honors at Arlington National Cemetery.

Admiral Isoroku Yamamoto

Admiral Yamamoto, architect of the Pearl Harbor attack, lived to see his predictions of Japanese defeats in the Pacific War come true. At Midway, the Americans sank four of his large carriers. Two months later, U.S. forces invaded Japanese-occupied Guadalcanal in the Solomon Islands. There, U.S. intelligence deciphered a Japanese code message announcing Yamamoto's visit to Bougainville Island. On April 18, 1943 sixteen American P-38 fighters ambushed his party over Bougainville's coast. Yamamoto's bomber crashed into the jungle. Searchers found his body in the wreckage a few days later.

Vice Admiral Chuichi Nagumo

In spite of the overwhelming success of the attack, and strong entreaties from air commander Fuchida, Vice Admiral Nagumo refused to order a second strike on Pearl Harbor. Military historians have criticized his judgement, pointing out that this decision spared the Americans much further damage. Nagumo remained in command of the First Air Fleet until its destruction at the Battle of Midway. In the summer of 1944 he commanded the 6,100 man naval detachment on Saipan in the Marianas. On July 7th, two days before the island fell to the Americans, Nagumo killed himself with a pistol.

Fate of the Japanese Task Force

Thirty-one Japanese ships began the war in the Pacific at Pearl Harbor. Only one, a tanker, survived to surrender to the Allies. Four of the Hawaii Operation's six carriers were lost first. At the battle of Midway, U.S. carrier dive-bombers ambushed and sank the *Akagi, Kaga, Soryu,* and *Hiryu.* An American pilot who had been at Pearl Harbor noted the columns of black smoke from the burning Japanese carriers and remembered the *Arizona.*

The escort battleships *Hiei* and *Kirishima* fell next. Off Guadalcanal, *Hiei* succumbed to 85 shell hits from American cruisers and destroyers on November 13, 1942. Two nights later, in the same waters, nine 16-inch shells from the American battleship *Washington* sank the *Kirishima.*

An American submarine destroyed the aircraft carrier *Shokaku* near the Philippines.

Four months later, U.S. torpedo planes sank the last surviving Pearl Harbor carrier, *Zuikaku,* at the battle of Leyte Gulf. This fight also claimed the heavy cruiser *Chikuma,* and the light cruiser *Abukuma.*

Over the course of the war U.S. forces sank all of the nine destroyers used in the Pearl Harbor assault. The *Arare* fell to torpedoes from the American submarine, *Growler* on July 5, 1942. Next came *Kagero,* sunk in the Solomons on May 8, 1943 by U.S. Marine Corps aircraft. Torpedoes from U.S. submarine, *Redfin* sent *Akigumo* to the bottom off the Philippines on April 11, 1944.

Less than two months later, on July 9, 1944, the American submarine, *Harder,* sank *Tanikaze.* U.S. Task Force 77 destroyed *Shiranuhi* on October 27, 1944 during the Battle of

The heavy cruiser, *Tone,* (above) lies beached in Kure Harbor's shallow water in August 1945. Lacking resources to repair the ship so late in the war, the Japanese removed the crew and some equipment on July 28, 1945. They abandoned the cruiser a week later.

Leyte Gulf in the Philippines, and U.S. submarine *Sealion* torpedoed and sank *Urakaze* off Formosa on November 21, 1944.

On April 7, 1945 American aircraft forces sank the destroyers *Hamakaze, Isokaze,* and *Kasumi,* while they accompanied the giant battleship *Yamato* on its one-way suicide mission to attack U.S. invasion forces off Okinawa.

With the war drawing to a close, on July 24, 1945, aircraft from U.S. carriers raided Kure Harbor in Japan. Four bomb hits and seven near misses sank the heavy cruiser *Tone,* the last warship of the Pearl Harbor attack fleet.

102

First Air Fleet

Akagi

Sunk by U.S. dive-bombers at the battle of Midway, June 4, 1942

Kaga

Bombed and sunk by U.S. carrier aircraft at Midway, June 4, 1942

Hiryu

Destroyed by U.S. dive-bombers at Midway, June 4, 1942

Soryu

Bombed and sunk by U.S. aircraft at Midway, June 4, 1942

Shokaku

Sunk near the Philippines by the U.S. sub *Cavalla*, June 19, 1944

Zuikaku

Sunk by U.S. carrier planes at Leyte Gulf on October 25, 1944

Escort Force

Abukuma

Sunk by U.S. Army Air Force planes at Leyte Gulf, October 26, 1944

Chikuma

Torpedoed by U.S. carrier planes at Leyte Gulf, October 25, 1944

Hiei

Sunk by gunfire and bombing at Guadalcanal, November 13, 1942

Kirishima

Sunk by battleship gunfire at Guadalcanal, November 15, 1942

Tone

Bombed and sunk by U.S. carrier planes, Kure Harbor, July 24, 1945

Destroyers

Arare: torpedoed in Aleutians, 1942
Kagero: sunk in Solomons, 1943
Akigumo: torpedoed, Philippines, 1944
Tanikaze: torpedoed, Philippines, 1944
Urakaze: torpedoed, Formosa, 1944
Shiranuhi: sunk, Philippines, 1944
Hamakaze: sunk off Japan, 1945
Isokaze: sunk off Japan, 1945
Kasumi: sunk off Japan, 1945

Submarines

I-19—sunk off Makin, Nov. 25, 1943
I-21—sunk off Tarawa, Nov. 27, 1943
I-23—sunk off Oahu, Feb. 15, 1942

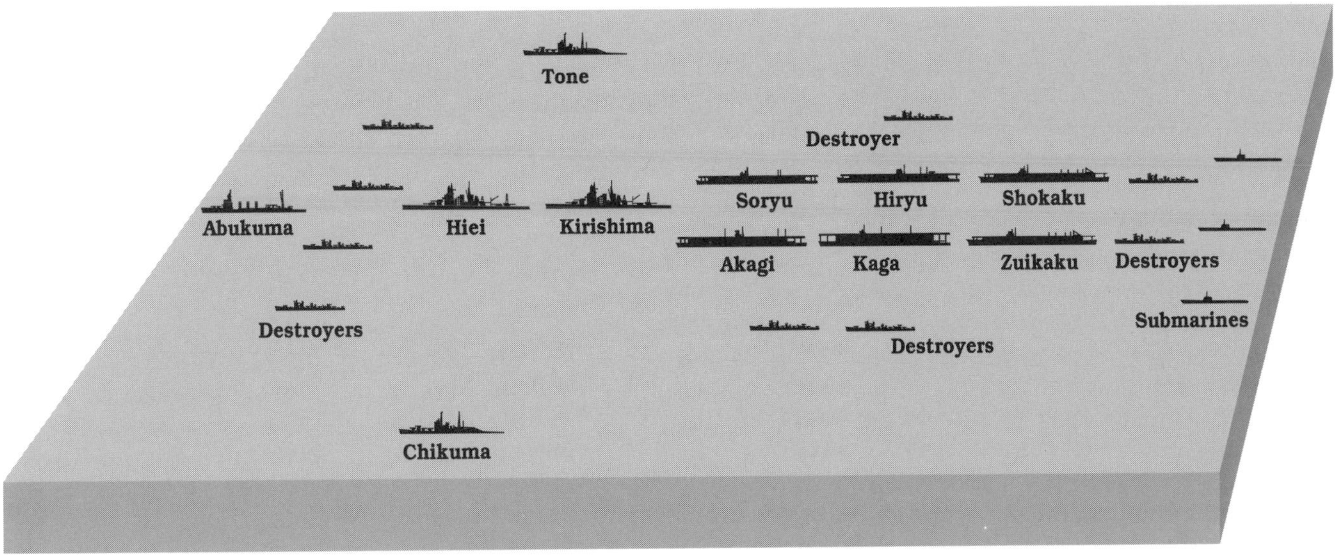

Survivors' Tales

Ensign H. D. Davison
USS *Arizona*

It was just before colors, in fact, I had already sent the messenger down to make the 8 o'clock reports to the captain. Then I heard a dive-bomber attack from overhead. I looked through my spyglass and saw the red dots on the wings. That made me wonder, but I still couldn't believe it until I saw some bombs falling.

The first one hit up by the air station. I sounded the air raid alarm and notified the captain. The captain and Lt. Comdr. Fuqua came on deck, and the captain went on up to the bridge. Mr. Fuqua told me to sound General Quarters.

About that time we took a bomb hit on the starboard side of the quarterdeck, just about abreast of No. 4 Turret. We grabbed the men available and started dropping the deck hatches and loading out hoses on the quarterdeck.

About this time, the planes that had made the initial dive-bomb attack strafed the ship. Mr. Fuqua and I told all hands to get in the marine compartment. It was reported to us that we had a bomb in the executive officers' office. Mr. Fuqua told me to call the center engine room and get pressure on the fire mains. Then he went up to the boat deck. I told the boatswain's mate of the watch to do that. Then I went into the O.D.'s booth to do it myself.

Just after I stepped in the booth, we took another hit which seemed to be on the starboard side of the quarterdeck, just about frame 88. The boatswain's mate and I were trapped in the booth by the flames. We started out, trying to run through the flames aft on the quarterdeck. We couldn't get through so we went over the lifeline into the water. I was conscious of a sweetish,

sickening smell to the flame. After I got in the water, my first intention was to go to the quay and then onto the quarterdeck, or swim to the gangway and get aboard. But after I took one look at the ship, I decided it was useless; she had settled down by the bow, and appeared broken in two. The foremast was toppled over; she was a mass of flames from the forecastle to just forward of Turret 3.

I was helped into a motor launch by Ensign Bush and another man. Then we in turn took the motor launch and picked up as many survivors as we could find in the water. We took them over to the landing at Ford Island. There we were met by air station marines, who helped us get the wounded ashore. . . . Then I went up to the dispensary for first aid.

J. A. Doherty, CGM
USS *Arizona*

I was in the chief's quarters when the air raid alarm sounded. At the same time I heard something hit. I went immediately to my battle station, which is the A.A. Battery. When I arrived on the boat deck, I saw the forecastle waving up and down, and fire and smoke coming up through seams of the deck.

I went to the starboard side. . . . I noticed No. 3 gun wasn't firing due to safety bearing when the foot firing mechanism cut out. I was then shocked and surrounded by smoke and flames. I was backing away from the smoke and I can't remember much from then on.

I was in the water and was helped in a boat and from there to a hospital.

104

Aviation Machinist's Mate, Third Class, M. T. Hurst
USS *Arizona*

. . . I watched several planes sweep over Ford Island and when one went over our fantail I saw the red spot on the wing. Our guns then opened up and it first struck me that we were being attacked. I went back on the quarterdeck and just as I reached the armor deck, General Quarters was sounded. . . .

When I reached main deck there was a fire in the Executive Officer's office. Lane, an aviation radioman, Burns, our yeoman, and I started to get a hose to fight the fire. At this time a fire broke out on the quarter deck, and we dragged the hose out there. Lane screwed on the nozzle while I went to turn on the water at the plug forward of No. 3 Turret.

A bomb hit somewhere forward of me and knocked me down. I finished turning on the water and started out to where I was to help Lane, but he was no longer there. I noticed there was no water coming out of the nozzle so I started to go forward and saw many marines and sailors lying about the deck badly burned. I tried to help one but he was pretty well blown up.

Someone yelled, "Get out of here," so I picked up someone and started to carry him off. Someone said to let him go since he was dead. It was pretty hot then and several men were running around badly burned, so with a couple of other fellows, one of them Burns, I helped to get these men over to the life line and told them to go over the side. I then went over to the blister and jumped into the water. . . . My shoes got separated from me someplace. . . . I swam to the motor launch tied up alongside of the quay.

Ensign G. S. Flannigan
USS *Arizona*

About 8 o'clock I heard the air raid siren. I was in the bunk room, and everyone in the room thought it was a joke to have an air raid on Sunday. Then I heard an explosion. I was undressed. I climbed into some khaki clothing and shoes. Then the general alarm bell went.

I made for my General Quarters station. I don't remember any word passed over the speaker system. My station was the lower room of Turret 3.

Just as the men and I got down the ladder leading to the passageway between the lower rooms of Turrets 3 and 4, a bomb exploded. The lights went out. It seemed to be on the third deck, starboard side between Turrets 3 and 4. When that bomb hit, it made a whish with a gust of hot air, and sparks flew. There followed a very nauseating gas and smoke immediately afterwards.

Before this time, Condition Zed had been set in the lower rooms of Turret 3, and the men in the passage and I were unable to get out of the passageway. I beat on the door for some minutes before someone inside the turret opened the door.

We got all the men we could find in the passageway into the lower room, and then dogged down the door. We were unable to dog down the door of the port passageway between 3 and 4 because it had been sprung by an explosion.

The air in the turret was fairly clear for a while, but finally gas or smoke started coming in. The men made quite a bit of confusion at first, but they were very obedient when Ensign Field and I ordered them to keep quiet.

About this time we got a flashlight and saw the turret was very misty with smoke. Just after this, we heard hissing

noise which was later discovered to be air leaking from holes in the forward transverse bulkhead of the lower room.

Ensign Field tried to get central station on the ship's service phone, but the phones were out. . . . Conditions from smoke were getting worse and worse. It was then we decided we would have to leave the lower room.

We sent men up the ladder to open the hatches to the electric deck, shell room, and pits. The men had difficulty opening the first hatch. Men were coughing badly when it was finally opened. We sent them up to the pits on the double.

There were two men and Ensign Field and I left in the lower room when water entered. It was about eight inches deep when Ensign Field and I finally left. We were the last two up. We climbed the ladder, closing all the hatches behind us.

I took charge of the men in the pits, and Ensign Field went out on deck to help Lt. Comdr. Fuqua. We saw smoke entering the pits through the pointers' and trainers' telescope slots. I urged the men to take off their shirts, and we closed the openings with some clothes.

After a short time, we got word from Ensign Field to come out on deck. . . . The ship seemed to be ablaze from the boat deck forward. We unlashed the life raft on the starboard side of Turret 3, and threw it in the water. I sent the men aboard the raft and shoved it off.

I was called aft, and helped wounded men in the barge leaving for Ford Island, and helped men to the front of the air raid shelter. . . . By this time the ship was ablaze from forward of Turret 3 to the bow. There were no boats to make another trip when I returned to the landing. I went into the air raid shelter.

Survivors' Tales

Comdr. W. F. Fitzgerald, Jr
USS Maryland

I was the regularly assigned staff duty officer on the morning of 7 December 1941. . . . Shortly before 8 o'clock I was undressed, ready to take a bath when I became conscious of intermittent explosions. I quickly got into my trousers and grabbed a hat and blouse and started for the topside. I was hardly out of my room when General Quarters was sounded.

I proceeded immediately to the Flag Bridge, telling all men I encountered to man their battle stations and to be calm. Upon arrival on topside, which I estimate to be about 8 o'clock, I noticed smoke, flame and many explosions throughout the harbor. I believe I heard machine gun fire from the *Maryland*. . . . I am conscious of having seen the *Oklahoma* upright but with a perceptible list to port. My first glance did not indicate to me that she was rolling over.

Heavy explosions continued. Upon arrival on the Flag Bridge I immediately checked with Captain Godwin to see if he was making all preparations for getting underway. He said he was. Captain W. R. Carter, Chief of Staff, said, "We can't do much good up here. Let's go down to the guns and give them a hand." We both proceeded to the 5-inch AA batteries and split up, each doing what he could to assist in organizing the gun crews, ammunition parties, and assigning to stations men who were not otherwise engaged. During all this the flame, smoke, and noise were terrific. . . .

Shortly after my arrival at the guns, the *Oklahoma* rolled over. Numerous men from the *Oklahoma* swam to the *Maryland* and upon coming aboard I assigned them gun stations or details in the ammunition party.

After the gun crews were organized and in action and under command of their own battery officers, I returned to the Flag Bridge. A great number of bombs were still falling. A terrific explosion took place on what I thought was the stern of the *Tennessee* but which I have since learned was the *Arizona*. A large fire was in progress on the *West Virginia*.

It was about this time I noted the *Nevada* was underway and standing down the channel. She seemed to be in good shape until about the time she arrived abreast of the Ten-Ten Dock at which time she was heavily bombed. She later turned around in the channel and was apparently aground.

Up until this time I cannot definitely state that I saw any formation of enemy planes. However, I did see numerous planes which seemed to be conducting single dive-bombing attacks.

While on the starboard side of the Flag Bridge I felt the *Maryland* shudder from what was apparently a near miss off the port bow. Within a second or two I saw a bomb land on the forecastle of the *Maryland*, and shortly thereafter (a matter of a few seconds) a large geyser of water sprung on the starboard bow, apparently from another near miss.

Within a few minutes a dive-bombing attack was noted coming in the port side across the forecastle of the *Maryland* at an altitude which appeared to be at the lowest point not over 200–250 feet. There were six or seven planes in this particular attack. One of the planes burst into flames and crashed from what I believe was a direct hit from the starboard battery of the *Maryland*. This was followed in a few moments by another plane which was shot down over Ford Island but which apparently was not in flames.

About this time I noticed a bombing attack on ships in the north channel. One of the planes in flame apparently landed directly on the *Curtiss*. By this time the guns of both the port and starboard batteries were firing continuously at the enemy planes. The ships seemed to be recovering from the shock of the original surprise and performing excellently.

The fires on the *Arizona* and *West Virginia* seemed to be increasing, and frequently the *Maryland* was entirely covered with heavy black smoke. In the meantime, various officers of the staff had reported back on board and immediately taken their stations. As near as I can remember I saw Commander Battleships on the Flag Bridge for the first time about 0905.

I cannot speak too highly of the conduct of the men during the entire action. There was no panic whatever. As I went from gun to gun and ammunition party to ammunition party I noted that even though there might have been surprise and fear present, every man was willing and anxious do his bit and after only a word or two of encouragement turned to his task with zest and efficiency.

Various tugs, lighters, and small boats were directed by Commander Battleships to proceed to the *West Virginia* and *Arizona* to assist in putting out the fire. In addition, rescue parties were sent to the *Oklahoma*—now rolled over about 150 degrees—in order to cut holes in the bottom and rescue the men who were trapped inside.

Comdr. R. H. Hillenkoetter
USS *West Virginia*

I was in my cabin commencing to dress, when at 0755 the word was passed "Away Fire and Rescue Party." This was followed by General Quarters. At the same time, the Marine orderly rushed into the cabin and announced, "The Japanese are attacking us." Two heavy shocks on the hull of the *West Virginia* were felt. . . .

By this time I had reached the quarterdeck, and the ship was beginning to list rapidly to port. I proceeded along the starboard side until just forward No. 3 Turret, when there was a third heavy shock felt to port. The planes on top of Turret 3 caught on fire, and there were flames all around the turret top. . . .

There was another heavy explosion that threw me flat on the deck.

The ship continued to list to port, and at the time of this latest shock, I estimate the list was 20 or 25 degrees. Immediately following this explosion, I saw a flash of flame about fifteen feet high somewhere forward on the *Arizona*, and had just gotten to my feet again when there was a terrific flash of flame from the *Arizona*, this second flash higher than the foretop. Burning debris of sizes from a fraction of an inch up to five inches in diameter rained on the quarterdeck of the *West Virginia*.

The ship's batteries continued firing, and shortly after the *Arizona* explosion, the list on the *West Virginia* stopped and she gradually started to right herself. Efforts to push overboard the burning embers on the quarterdeck and to

extinguish the fire on top of Turret 3 and in the planes continued. There was another heavy shock, distinguishable from the shock of the ship's own guns firing. . . . A large fire had broken out amidships. . . .

A telephone talker said "Central Station says Abandon Ship." As it was evident the fire fighting party had no chance to extinguish the fire, they were ordered to leave. The fire had, from all appearances, isolated the after and forward parts of the ship.

By this time the stern of the *Tennessee* was burning, and a wall of flame was advancing toward the *West Virginia* from oil on the water from the *Arizona*. I looked around and saw no one else aft on deck and then I dove overboard and swam to the *Tennessee*.

Survivors' Tales

Lt. Comdr. William M. Hobby
USS *Oklahoma*

On the morning of Sunday, December 7, 1941 the *Oklahoma* was secured at Berth F-5, Pearl Harbor, outboard of the *Maryland.* Commander J. L. Kenworthy was senior officer on board, and I was second in command. At about 0800 I heard the word over the loud-speaker to man the anti-aircraft battery, then shots from an indeterminate direction, then a second time the word to man the anti-aircraft battery for a real attack.

As I was going topside, the word was passed to man all battle stations. I ran up the starboard side out to the main deck aft by the break of the deck. Before I reached the main deck aft there was a din of gunfire and explosions from all directions.

I started up the ladder from the main deck aft to the anti-aircraft gun platform on the starboard side; at this point I felt what I believe was the first torpedo hit—a dull thud and a powerful reverberation on the port side, and the ship began listing to port.

I started back down with the idea of getting to Central and directing the flooding of the starboard blisters, but almost immediately there was a second torpedo hit and then a third, and the ship listed more.

At this time, streams of men were pouring up through the hatches to topside. A second or so later, at about the time I was back down to the main deck aft again, came the fourth torpedo hit, and the ship continued to list to port—at least a 20 degree list at this time, I estimate.

I directed petty officers near me to spread out over the length of the ship and keep the men as orderly and calm as possible.

I sighted Commander Kenworthy on the starboard catwalk and made my way to him and told him I thought the best now was to save as many men as possible, that it was now impossible to make further watertight closures and establish any further watertight integrity. He agreed and we both passed the word to abandon ship. I called to men on main deck aft to attempt to get to work on the loud-speaker.

Although there were now hundreds of men on the starboard side, the general conduct of all hands was quiet and calm. There was an explosion around the port side of the forecastle, which I thought was a bomb hit.

I worked my way forward and Commander Kenworthy worked his way aft. There was another shock and concussion and vibration, and fuel oil splashed in streams over everything topside. This was either another torpedo hit or a large bomb hit close aboard.

The ship continued to list over to port, now about 30 degrees or more, I thought. I entered No. 1 casemate to see about the escape of men from below to topside. Men were still coming out through the casemates, and thence out through gun ports to the catwalk and onto the side.

When no more men were to be seen in casemates, I climbed up through a gun port and out over the side. The ship was capsizing and the angle was about 90 degrees. I pulled myself along the side and bottom as the vessel keeled over. The ship finally settled when the mast and stack hit bottom, with an angle of approximately 145 degrees, starboard side uppermost.

I saw on the bottom at about frame 60, hundreds of men were along the hull, making their way to the water's edge. C. W. Keenum,

CBM, joined me and rendered much aid in steadying the men and directing them to swim to the *Maryland,* to the Ford Island Landing, or to a motor launch, depending on [their] location. The air attack continued and bombs were dropping nearby, but none struck the *Oklahoma* after she capsized.

All men who reached the topside were apparently saved. . . . There were many cases of men aiding others to swim, and in some cases, actually towing them to the shore. . . . I saw Boatswain Bothne acting as coxwain of a motor launch and picking up men and taking them to Ford Island landing.

After all others had cleared the hull of the ship, as far as we could see, Keenum and I made our way out to the bow. I discarded shoes and uniform, expecting to swim in. At this juncture Botswain Bothne approached in a motor launch, having already landed one load of men. . . .

I remained in the motor launch, and with Boatswain Bothne and four men, patrolled up and down the line facing the *Oklahoma, West Virginia,* and *Arizona,* looking for survivors. By this time it appeared all men had reached shore. We patrolled for about twenty minutes, until it seemed the attack was over, or at least that no more bombs were being dropped, and we could see no more enemy planes. . . .

I commandeered a motor boat and returned to the hull of the *Oklahoma.* Others were on the *Oklahoma* and still more were coming aboard as I arrived. With several men I went over the hull discussing possibilities of salvaging those still alive inside. . . . I remained on the hull for the next sixty hours as senior *Oklahoma* officer.

Chief Machinist, Second Class, W. F. Staff
USS *Oklahoma*

Sunday morning at 0750 on 7 December 1941, I was in the Carpenter Shop when the general alarm was sounded. I immediately went along the starboard side of the third deck to my battle station. I felt several explosions on the way to Repair II. When I got to Repair II, I took my phones and went to get a flashlight, but they were locked up so I went down to A-28, the forward air compressor room, and started to set Zed.

There was an electrician's mate and a fireman, also J. P. Centers, MM, 2nd class, and myself in the compartment. When the lights went out, the fireman and electrician's mate started to go out the Zed hatch which had been set by Repair II; they were yelling and screaming. Water and fuel oil was coming down the hatch. I tried to stop them from opening the hatch but couldn't.

The next thing we knew we were all under water and oil. Centers and myself were the only ones that came up. It took us some time in the dark to find out we were back in A-28 and the ship had capsized.

We then tried to get into the linen storeroom. It was on the starboard side and was out of the water. A-28 was about half full of oil and water. The storeroom was locked and it took several hours to beat the lock off with a wrench we found on the air compressor. We could not get into the storeroom, as gear must have wedged against the door.

We tried to get into a small storeroom which was on the overhead, but it was also locked and we could not get into position to beat the lock off.

About Monday noon we heard tapping and we answered them. After so long they were right overhead and we could hear them talking. When they started to cut into us, it let out our air and we were under air pressure; the water came up as our air escaped.

The water came up and ran out the hole they were cutting and they left. But we still had about six inches of air space. We tried the linen room again and it gave a little. Apparently the water had cleared the gear from the door. We went in and started tapping again. The rescuers soon got out to us again and we left the ship at 0200 Tuesday morning.

Survivors' Tales

Lt. Comdr. M. N. Little
USS *California*

About 0750 or 0755, Sunday December 7, 1941, I was working in my office when I heard a series of explosions followed by the word passed over the loudspeaker system, "Air raid! Air raid! Seek shelter! Séek shelter!" I rushed from my office . . . As I reached the emergency platform I heard several heavy explosions and looking aft saw large columns of water arising along the ships moored abaft the *California.*

Lt. Fritschmann was in control of the ship's armament. I ordered him to complete the manning of the A. A. Battery, as soon as possible to get up ammunition, and open fire on any enemy planes sighted. I ordered Main Control to make preparations for getting underway.

. . .Within a few minutes I saw a low flying plane approach from the direction of Merry Point, bank steeply, and launch a torpedo. The bubble track of the torpedo was clearly visible as it headed for us and struck the ship somewhere slightly abaft the port beam about frame 100. As the torpedo exploded, a column of water arose along the port side and the ship lurched and began to list to port. . . .

After the first torpedo hit it was reported that power was lost on the A. A. hoists, and I directed the ammunition supply be started using hand power. Central Station reported counterflooding was in progress and the list had apparently been checked, at least temporarily, when the second torpedo struck.

I caught only a glimpse through the conning tower eye port of the track of the second torpedo as it approached, but believe it struck forward of amidships, about a-beam of Turret No. 2. . . . The list

Private A. E. Senior
USS *California*

When General Quarters was sounded I went to my battle station, 5-inch/51 Gun No. 8 in Casemate No. 8 on the port side. The battery officer asked for volunteers to go below for gas masks. I volunteered, but we could not get down to the storeroom where the masks were stored, so we returned to our gun stations. Again the battery officer asked for two volunteers to go below and haul 5-inch/25 A.A. ammunition to the topside because the hoists were out of commission.

We went down through the escape hatch in Casemate No. 6, through the Division Compartment, and finally through the hatch on the starboard side to the C-L Division Compartment. This is where ammunition was being taken out of the hoist which was being operated by hand in the handling room. It was being passed from there to the topside by hand.

It was here, at this time I first saw Ensign H. C. Jones. He was standing on the third deck at the foot of the ladder directing the hand passing of ammunition. I was at the top of the ladder from the handling room, and only one man was between myself and Ensign Jones.

We had been down there about fifteen or twenty minutes when the bomb hit on the starboard side of the ship. The only light we had was blown out. When it hit, the compartment filled with smoke and I reached for my gas mask, which I had laid on top of a shell box behind me. Then someone said, "Mr. Jones has been hit" so I flashed the flashlight I had on Ensign Jones' face and it was all bloody. His white coat also had blood all over it.

Two other men and myself took hold of Mr. Jones and started up the ladder with him. We got him as far as the M Division Compartment. Then he wouldn't let us carry him any farther. When we tried to he said, "Leave me alone, I'm done for. Get out of here before the magazines go off." Then there was another shock from below and that's the last I remember until they were pulling me up through the escape hatch in Casemate No. 3.

after the second torpedo hit increased markedly and was about six or seven degrees. . . .

Just before the bombing attack, Commander Stone, the executive officer, appeared on the bridge, having returned to the ship from shore leave at 0845. I was with him when what appeared to be a whole stick of bombs landed on our starboard side in the water between the ship and the shore. A few seconds later the ship was hit by a bomb amidships on the starboard side. There was a heavy explosion below decks, followed by light smoke, and later heavy smoke. This bombing was followed by

strafing with machine guns. Such guns of our battery as had ammunition and could bear were in action.

. . . The fire was raging on the starboard side in the interior of the ship. . . . I started across to the port side, intending to try to get inside to the main deck but the fire on the next ship astern had worked down to the oil which formed a heavy coating on the surface of the water and was coming down rapidly toward the *California* with the wind which was blowing a fresh breeze from that direction. . . . The Captain directed the Executive Officer to order the crew to abandon ship.

Lt. Comdr. S. S. Isquith
USS *Utah*

On Sunday, December 7, 1941, while moored at Berth FOX-11, Pearl Harbor, three planes whose identification were not questioned but taken for U.S. planes maneuvering, were observed just as colors were being hoisted at 0800, heading northerly from the harbor entrance. They made a low dive on the southern end of Ford Island and each dropped a bomb.

Immediately thereafter the air was filled with planes clearly distinguished as yellow colored planes with brilliant red Rising Sun insignia on fuselage and red wing tips, flying low at about 100 knots speed and dropping aerial torpedoes and bombs. They appeared to be Henkle 113, or similar type, with very silent engines. The general alarm was immediately rung and word was passed, "All hands to bombing quarters."

About this time, 0801, a severe underwater hit, at approximately frame 84, port side, was felt and the ship immediately commenced to list to port. Another underwater hit was felt almost immediately

thereafter in about the same general location and the listing of the ship increased immediately to about 15 degrees. At this time I realized the ship would capsize, and word was passed. "All hands on deck and all engine room and fire room, radio and dynamo watch to lay up on deck and release all prisoners. . . ."

By about 0805, the ship had listed to about 40 degrees to port. Lights were still on. No report had been received from the dynamo room; word was again passed. "All hands on deck and abandon ship over starboard side."

The crew commenced getting over the side, the ship continuing to list but somewhat slower. The attacking planes were now returning from a northerly direction, flying low and strafing the crew as they abandoned ship. The loosed timbers about the decks were moving to port, interfering greatly with the efforts of the crew to abandon ship.

Observing the strafing and the moving of the timbers and loose gear in the air castles, I directed that the crew divide into three groups, one group going up the ladder leading from the starboard air castle to the captain's cabin,

one going up the ladder from the starboard wardroom to the passage inboard of the captain's stateroom, and one going up the ladder leading from the starboard near the wardroom pantry to the forecastle. A large number of these men escaped through the ports in the captain's cabin. Lt. P. F. Hauck, Machinist S. A. Szymanski, and myself were the last to leave the ship, going through the ports in the captain's cabin.

At this time, about 0810, the ship was listing about 80 degrees to port, and planes were still strafing the ship. Mooring lines were parting and two motor launches and the motor whale boat were picking up men in the water. Many men were observed swimming to the north and south quays of Pier FOX-11, and as planes were still strafing, the men were ordered to the sides of the quays for some protection.

At about 0812, the last mooring lines had parted and the ship was capsized, the keel plainly showing. All men picked up by ship's boats were taken ashore to Ford Island, and boats were ordered to return and pick up any men still swimming about.

Survivors' Tales

Seaman Earl Ronald Laster
USS *Nevada*

I was sitting on a mess bench in the M. Division compartment when General Quarters sounded. I started to my battle station when I heard machine gun fire and the hum of dive-bombers. Someone said the Japs were attacking, but I couldn't believe it. It was so unreal all the way through the battle.

I manned my battle station, a 5" ammunition hoist on the main deck in the after marine compartment. I could still hear the chatter of the machine guns and the loud blast of the bombs. The ship gave a great lurch every time she was hit. We were sending ammunition up as fast as the hoist would run. The AA battery was firing without interruptions. I was working so hard the fighting didn't scare me until we had a few minutes' breathing spell after the first attack had ended.

During this time we had cut all lines and got underweigh. The ship had two torpedoes in the bow and three bombs on the ship. One on the forecastle and two on the bridge. She was listing badly forward.

When the second attack came, we started putting shells in the hoist on the double again, and there was a great blast in the right compartment from ours that nearly knocked me over. The man standing in front of me was knocked against me and I caught him. A bomb had hit on the boat deck and come down through the galley. I was so scared I didn't know what, but we stayed there until the hoist was out of operation. The bomb had nicked the guns on the front side and killed and wounded better than fifty men.

We went into the right compartment forward and stood by

Earl Ronald Laster sent his journal to his great grandmother for safekeeping rather than allowing the Navy to censor it. The Pearl Harbor attack was the first action he saw as a seaman. On December 13, 1941 he was transferred to the carrier, *Lexington*, just five months before it was sunk at the Battle of the Coral Sea.

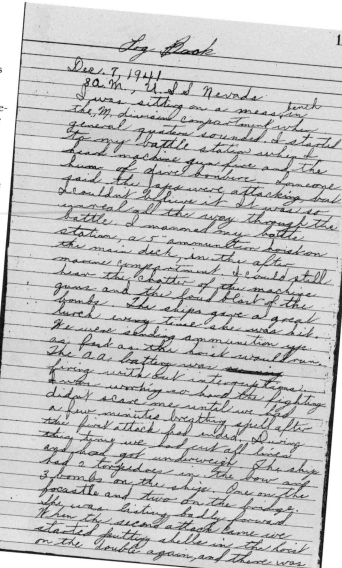

to help out with the wounded. Then the worst part of it all happened. The wounded came down through our compartment to get to the sick bay. Some had legs gone; others were blind and burnt so bad you couldn't help them. You just had to tell them which way to go. I helped several of them that could walk down the ladder. They were cut so bad from shrapnel they were just covered with blood.

During this time the second attack had been beaten off, and we were helping with most everything there was to do. The ship

had gone from our box to the shore just off Ford Island. It was listing so bad by that time we had to beach her. Some tugs pushed us on the beach.

I was helping to carry the dead down from the top side. . . . We worked the rest of the day. We worked at everything, just anything to keep busy. That night I got three hours of sleep although it was 130° in the engine rooms. I got up about twelve o'clock and got off the ship until Monday night late and when I finally got a mattress to lay on I never woke up until Tuesday morning late.

U.S. Naval Hospital

Page Cooper, in her book,
Navy Nurse, described what
happened at the U.S. Naval
Hospital just after the attack:

The wounded began to come. Those who were brought by water in ship's boats, launches, anything that would float, were carried directly into the hospital on stretchers. The hospital ambulances which had gone out at the first alarm drew up to the receiving station in the old nurses' quarters which were being demolished to make way for a pier. The building was nothing but a shell, no windows, no doors, but there was plenty of room. As fast as they could unload the ambulances, trucks, carts, and limousines, the corpsmen brought in the casualties and laid them on matresses spaced about on the floor. Most of them were from the ships in the harbor; boys with flesh torn by gunshot wounds, arms and legs blown off by bomb fragments, and above all, bodies covered with burns foul with thick black oil.

At the receiving station Freda Conine was part of a team that worked like a human conveyor belt. The receiving doctors examined the wounded, and a group of doctors and nurses gave them morphine to ease the pain. There was no time to boil the tablets for each injection. One nurse replenished the solution of morphine, another took care of the tray of hypodermic needles kept sterile in alcohol. Others gave first aid and tagged the patients, recording what treatment they had received and to which ward they were assigned. Corpsmen moved them on to the operating rooms, the wards. All of them were under high emotional tension, some of them hysterical

others sunk in a depression, many of them in shock. Before the mattresses had lost the warmth of their bodies, others had been laid in their places.

All morning the work went on. Most of the men who lay on the mattresses were covered with burns, flashburns from exploding shells, and oil burns. Although their clothes had often been torn or blasted away, she could tell what they had been wearing when the attack came. Those who were in shorts and no shirts were a total mass of burns—backs, chests, and abdomens—all except their thighs; on some the broiled flesh on the arms stopped at the line of the cap sleeves of their undershirts, making their arms look as though they were encased in mottled hideous sixteen-button opera gloves, while those who were wearing shirts and trousers escaped with singed hair and blistered hands and faces.

To these doctors and nurses straining to keep up with the flood of injured men, time ceased to exist. When Freda Conine saw a chow cart rolling down the bare, stained floor of the receiving shed, she glanced at her watch. It was exactly twelve o'clock. As the corpsman gave her a glass of orange juice and a bowl of soup, the thought flashed through her weary brain that she was witnessing a miracle. In the turmoil and hysteria of the bombing the galleys had managed to prepare a meal for many more than twice the usual number of patients and—this was the heart of the miracle—they had served chow on time.

That Sunday afternoon the doctors and nurses at the receiving station kept on without relief. In the wards the work went at the same relentless pace, and in the operating room the anesthetist and the supervisor of dressings tried to keep pace with four teams that worked at the same

time in four relays, a system which they were to maintain for three days. . . .

Before dark the windows of the operating room and one medication room had been painted black, but throughout the wards the nurses worked with blue paper over their flashlights. In the wards that housed the burn cases where the work went on, blackout or no blackout, the corpsmen pinned up blankets across the windows. The blankets shut out the air and shut in the odor of charred flesh.

No one went to bed that night. Fortunately the supplies did not give out; there was no shortage of dressings, and the corpsmen broke out water bottles by the truckload. In the restroom a dozen mattresses had been laid on the floor, and on these the nurses snatched a two-hour rest period in their uniforms, but it was impossible to sleep with machine guns popping outside somewhere in the dark. Rumors swept through the wards: paratroopers were creeping down from the hills to shut off the electric power and wreck the water mains. The Japs had made landings on the other side of the island and were marching on Honolulu. At the dressing carts, in the corridors, by the doors of the quiet rooms new stories passed in whispers from one to the other.

Occasionally one of the corpsmen took a jug of coffee to the doctor, the dentist, and the corpsman stationed at the landing to identify the dead. By morning this part of the grim business had been almost completed. The score of deaths added to a rough total which showed that the Navy had lost more men in three hours than during the whole of the first World War. The casualties admitted to the hospital exceeded five hundred.

Arizona Memorial

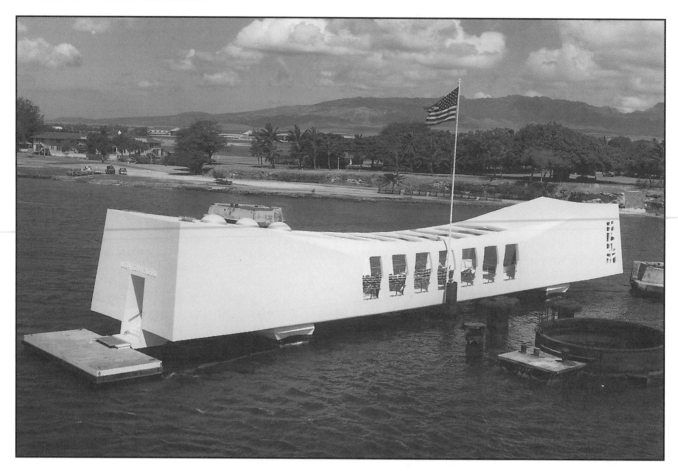

**Dedicated
to the Eternal Memory
of the
Gallant Shipmates
in the USS *Arizona* who
Gave Their Lives in Action
7 December 1941**

From today on the USS *Arizona* will again fly our country's flag just as proudly as she did on the morning of 7 December 1941. I am sure the *Arizona's* crew will know and appreciate what we are doing.

*Admiral A. W. Radford, USN
7 March 1950*

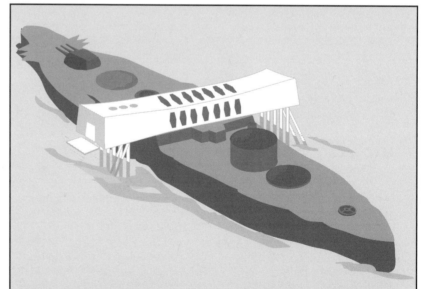

Wide opening in walls and roof permit a flooding by sunlight and a close view of the sunken battleship. . . At low tide, as the sun shines upon the hull, the barnacles which encrust it shimmer like gold jewels . . . a beautiful sarcophagus. The form, wherein the structure sags in the center but stands strong and vigorous at ends, expresses initial defeat and ultimate victory.
— *Alfred Preis, Architect*

In July 1942, following extensive surveys, the Pearl Harbor Navy Yard decided USS *Arizona* could not be salvaged. Washington accepted this conclusion, and after removal of the battleship's superstructure down to the main deck, the Navy, on December 1, 1942, erased *Arizona* from the list of commissioned ships. Navy vessels entering Pearl Harbor, however, continued to salute the wrecked battleship as a gesture of respect.

In 1950, Arthur Radford, commander of the Pacific Fleet, ordered the American flag flown on a small platform attached to *Arizona*. Eight years later, Congress approved legislation for a permanent *Arizona* memorial. The bill authorized construction "in honor and commemoration of the members of the Armed Forces of the United States who gave their lives to their country

during the attack on Pearl Harbor." The State of Hawaii and several veterans' organizations also contributed funds to the project.

The design award went to architect Alfred Preis' plan for an enclosed white marble bridge that spanned *Arizona's* hull and rested on two concrete girders sunk into the harbor bottom. No part of the 184 foot structure actually touched the ship. In a shrine room at the back of the

memorial are the names of the 1,177 *Arizona* crewmen killed when the ship sank. The monument was built over a four year period and dedicated on Memorial Day in 1962.

Approximately a million and a half people tour the site each year. An Arizona Memorial Visitor Center, administered by the National Park Service, was completed in 1980 and serves as a museum, interpretive center, and departure point for visitors.

Perspective underwater survey bow and stern views of the USS *Arizona* (below). Within a week after the attack, divers began exploring the *Arizona* to assess its condition. They found the forward magazine explosion had vented

through the deck in front of Turret No. 1, blowing the ship sides almost horizontal in this area. Divers moving into the interior of the ship discovered the main and second decks blocked with wreckage forward of frame 76. Gun Turrets Nos. 1 and 2

collapsed in the explosion. The Navy finished its salvage work on the *Arizona* in October 1943. In 1983, the National Park Service, in order to better manage the memorial, set its Submerged Cultural Resource Unit to mapping the remains of the USS *Arizona*. Over a five-year period, the Park Service surveyed

the wreck, assessed its condition, and formulated plans to better preserve it. Its report concluded, "The USS *Arizona* and the *Arizona* Memorial have become a major shrine not only for the lost battleship, but also for the entire attack." *Drawings by Jerry Livingston, National Park Service.*

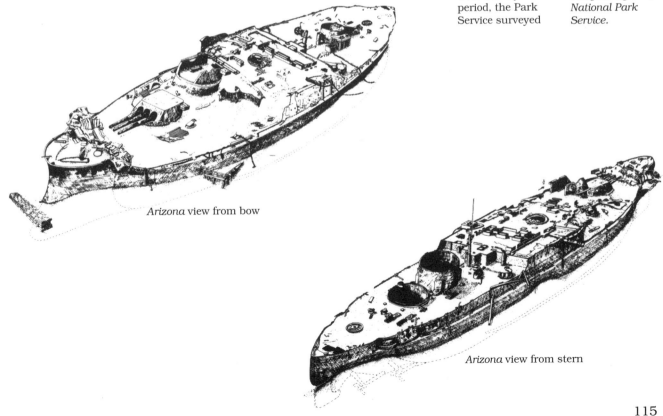

Arizona view from bow

Arizona view from stern

Utah Memorial

On December 23, 1909, the U.S. Navy launched USS *Utah*, its second dreadnought battleship. This new ship displaced 21,825 tons, could steam at 20 knots and bristled with ten 12-inch main battery guns and sixteen 5-inch second battery guns. Twelve-inch armor protected the ship's vitals and the thousand man crew.

In 1914, USS *Utah* supported the American landing at Vera Cruz, Mexico during the Mexican Civil War. In an action in April 1914, seven members of the *Utah*'s crew distinguished themselves and received medals of honor. The battleship ended World War I by escorting President Woodrow Wilson's ship to the Versailles Peace Conference.

In 1931 the Navy converted the aging battleship to a remote-controlled target vessel assigned to the Pacific Fleet. For the next four years Navy planes and warships practiced their fighting skills using USS *Utah* as a moving target.

The ship's role changed again in 1935 when it became an antiaircraft training ship. Sailors from the Pacific Fleet used *Utah*'s 5-inch guns, 1.1-inch antiaircraft guns, and 50 caliber machine guns to practice their antiaircraft skills.

USS *Utah* spent the last six weeks of its commissioned life holding advanced antiaircraft firing practice in Hawaiian waters. *Utah* returned to Pearl Harbor for the weekend of December 6–7 and moored at Berth F-11 at Ford Island. On Sunday December 7th at 8 a.m. Japanese planes attacked the *Utah* with torpedoes. Two or three exploded on the battleship's port side. When the ship listed to 15 degrees, the senior office aboard, Lt. Comdr. S. S. Isquith, ordered all hands on deck. Four minutes later *Utah* listed at 40 degrees and he gave the order to abandon ship. USS *Utah* capsized at 8:12 a.m.

Men scrambled into the water amid continuous Japanese strafing. Banging from *Utah*'s upturned hull attracted the attention of three of the ship's crew, and even before the attack ended they used a cutting torch to rescue a trapped sailor. Six officers and 52 enlisted men from a crew of 500 men lost their lives aboard the USS *Utah*. On December 29, 1941 salvage teams began their survey of the battleship.

In November 1942 the Navy completed its damage assessment of USS *Utah* (left). Pearl Harbor Salvage drew on its experience with the capsized battleship, USS *Oklahoma*, and decided to use a similar system of electric winches and steel cables to right the *Utah*. Workers removed ordnance and the ship's oil supply in January 1943. Over the next twelve months the winches managed to pull *Utah* onto its side, but were unable to go further. In March 1944 the Navy decided *Utah* could not be salvaged and abandoned the effort with the ship (below) resting on its side at a 38 degree angle. *Drawing by Jerry Livingston, National Park Service.*

The USS *Utah* Memorial (top opposite) with Ford Island in the background.

Utah is located a mile from the USS *Arizona* Memorial on the opposite side of Ford Island. The ship rests on its port side with the deck facing the channel. A portion of *Utah's* starboard side amidships rises from the water and is visible from the island. The port side torpedo holes which sank the ship are buried in the harbor's silt. In 1972 the Navy dedicated the USS *Utah* Memorial. It is a simple platform and flagstaff connected to Ford Island by a 70-foot walkway. A Naval honor guard raises the colors each morning to honor the *Utah*.

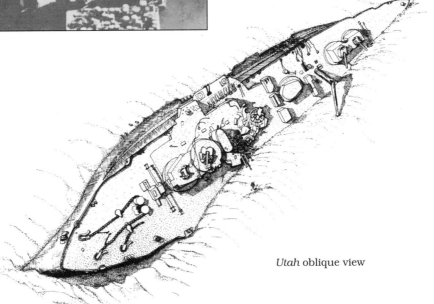

Utah oblique view

Aerial view of Pearl Harbor in 1942, looking from Pearl City southward past Ford Island to the mouth of the harbor.

Summary of Losses

U.S. Ship Losses

Arizona	battleship	**total loss; sunk**—eight heavy bomb hits
Oklahoma	battleship	**total loss; capsized and sunk**—five or more torpedo hits
West Virginia	battleship	**sunk; later raised and repaired**—five to seven torpedo hits; two bomb hits
California	battleship	**sunk; later raised and repaired**—two torpedo hits; one large bomb hit; one or more bomb near misses
Nevada	battleship	**heavy damage; beached and later repaired**—one torpedo hit; at least five bomb hits; two bomb near misses
Pennsylvania	battleship	**moderate damage; repaired**—one bomb hit
Maryland	battleship	**moderate damage; repaired**—two bomb hits
Tennessee	battleship	**moderate damage; repaired**—two bomb hits
Utah	target ship	**total loss; capsized and sunk**—two or three torpedo hits
Helena	light cruiser	**heavy damage; repaired**—one torpedo hit
Honolulu	light cruiser	**moderate damage; repaired**—one bomb near miss
Raleigh	light cruiser	**heavy damage; repaired**—one torpedo hit; one bomb hit
Shaw	destroyer	**heavy damage; repaired**—three bomb hits
Cassin	destroyer	**damaged beyond repair**—one direct bomb hit; secondary explosions caused by depth charges
Downes	destroyer	**damaged beyond repair**—two direct bomb hits; secondary explosions caused by depth charges and torpedoes
Helm	destroyer	**moderate damage; repaired**—near miss from bomb
Vestal	repair ship	**heavy damage; repaired**—two bomb hits
Oglala	mine-layer	**sunk; salvaged and repaired**—one torpedo which passed under the ship and exploded against the *Helena*
Curtiss	seaplane tender	**heavy damage; repaired**—one bomb hit; Japanese plane out of

U.S. Aircraft Losses

Bellows Field	3 planes
Ewa Marine Corps Air Station	33 planes
Ford Island Naval Air Station	26 planes
Hickam Field	18 planes
Kaneohe Naval Air Station	28 planes
Wheeler Field	53 planes
USS *Enterprise*	10 planes
Total:	**171 planes**

U.S. Casualties

	Killed	Wounded
Navy	1,998	710
Army	233	364
Marines	109	69
Civilians	48	35
Total:	**2,388**	**1,178**

Japanese Losses

Aircraft

Fighters	9		
Dive-bombers	15		
Torpedo bombers	5	**Total:**	**29**

Submarines

Large I-class subs	1		
Midget subs	5	**Total:**	**6**

Casualties

Airmen	55		
Large I-class sub	121		
Midget sub crew	9	**Total:**	**185**

Chronology

Aug. 1937   Japanese troops (below) invade Shanghai. The Chinese defend the city for three months, causing high Japanese casualties.

Aug. 1939   Admiral Isoroku Yamamoto assumes command of the Japanese Combined Fleet.

May 1940   Japanese Navy holds large-scale training exercises in preparation for the Southern Operation—the conquest of Southeast Asia.

Sept. 1940   Japan signs the Tripartite Pact, aligning with Nazi Germany and Italy.

Jan. 1941   Yamamoto proposes an attack on Pearl Harbor as part of the Southern Operation.

Feb. 1941   Admiral Husband E. Kimmel takes command of the United States Pacific Fleet.

March 1941   The Japanese prepare plans for Operation Hawaii—the Pearl Harbor attack.

March 8, 1941   U.S. Congress approves the Roosevelt administration's Lend-Lease Bill to provide aid to countries that oppose the Fascist powers.

April 1941   The United States begins Lend-Lease support to China which has been under Japanese attack since 1937.

July 24, 1941   Japan invades Indochina.

July 26, 1941   The United States freezes Japanese assets and cuts off oil exports to Japan.

Aug. 1941   Japan negotiates with the U.S. for removal of sanctions and restoration of vital petroleum supplies.

Sept. 6, 1941   Japanese Imperial Conference decides to go to war with the United States, Great Britain, and the Netherlands if negotiations are not successful within a month.

U.S. intercepts intelligence between Tokyo and the Japanese Consulate-General in Honolulu, asking spies to report positions of U.S. ships at Pearl Harbor.

Sept. 24, 1941

General Hideki Tojo (left) is appointed prime minister of Japan, and forms War Cabinet.

Oct. 1941

Admiral Yamamoto orders the attack on Pearl Harbor.

Nov. 5 1941

The First Air Fleet, commanded by Vice Admiral Chuichi Nagumo, leaves Japan's Kurile Islands for Pearl Harbor.

Nov. 26 1941

Emperor Hirohito and the Privy Council of Japan authorize the attack on Pearl Harbor.

Dec. 1 1941

USS *Condor* spots a Japanese submarine periscope near the mouth of Pearl Harbor.

*Dec. 7, 1941
3:50 a.m.*

USS *Ward* sinks a midget submarine outside the harbor entrance.

*Dec. 7, 1941
6:40 a.m.*

Operation Hawaii, the Pearl Harbor attack, begins. Three hundred fifty Japanese planes, in two waves, bomb and strafe U.S. ships in Pearl Harbor and air bases at Ford Island, Hickam, Wheeler, Kaneohe, Bellows, and Ewa.

*Dec. 7, 1941
7:55 a.m.*

The attack ends. Japanese aircraft return to their carriers.

*Dec. 7, 1941
9:45 a.m.*

Japan officially declares war on the U.S. and Great Britain.

*Dec. 7, 1941
10:30 a.m.*

Japan attacks Hong Kong, the Philippines, and British Malaya.

Dec. 7, 1941

The United States declares war on Japan. President Franklin D. Roosevelt (right) makes the declaration to Congress and the nation.

Dec. 8, 1941

Bibliography

This bibliography includes books consulted in the preparation of *The Attack on Pearl Harbor: An Illustrated History,* as well as titles that may be of further interest to the reader.

Allen, Gwenfread. *Hawaii's War Years.* Honolulu: University of Hawaii Press, 1950.

Barker, A. J. *Pearl Harbor.* Illustrated Battle History of World War II, no. 10. New York: Ballantine Books, 1969.

Burlingame, Burl. *Advance Force Pearl Harbor.* Kailua, Hawaii: Pacific Monograph, 1992.

Carpenter, Dorr, and Norman Polmar. *Submarines of the Imperial Japanese Navy.* Annapolis: Naval Institute Press, 1986.

Cohen, Stan. *East Wind Rain.* Missoula, Montana: Pictorial Histories Publishing Co., 1981.

Cooper, Page. *Navy Nurse.* New York: McGraw-Hill Book Company, Inc., 1946.

Dull, Paul S. *A Battle History of the Imperial Japanese Navy (1941–1945).* Annapolis: Naval Institute Press, 1978.

Friedman, Norman. *U.S. Cruisers.* Annapolis: Naval Institute Press, 1984.

Friedman, Norman, Arthur D. Baker, III, Arnold S. Lott, and Robert F. Sumrall. *USS Arizona.* Ship's Data, no. 3. Annapolis: Leeward Publications, 1978.

Garzke, William H., Jr., and Robert O. Dulin, Jr. *Battleships.* Annapolis: Naval Institute Press, 1985.

Hata, Ikuhiko, and Yasuho Izawa. *Japanese Naval Aces and Fighter Units in World War II.* Translated by Don Cyril Gorham. Annapolis: Naval Institute Press, 1989.

Ienaga, Saburo. *The Pacific War.* New York: Pantheon Books, 1978.

Jane's Fighting Ships. Annual Volumes. New York: Macmillan Company, 1936–1941.

Joint Committee on the Investigation of the Pearl Harbor Attack. *Pearl Harbor Attack: Hearings before the Congress of the United States.* Parts 1–39. Washington, D. C.: U.S. Government Printing Office, 1946.

Krejcarek, Kevin K., ed. *Hickam: The First Fifty Years.* Hickam AFB, Hawaii: Public Affairs Division, 1985.

Larkins, William T. *U.S. Navy Aircraft 1921–1941.* Concord, California: Aviation History Publications, 1961.

Layton, Edwin T., with Roger Pineau, and John Costello. *"And I Was There."* New York: William Morrow and Co., 1985.

Lenihan, Daniel J., ed. *Submerged Cultural Resources Study.* Southwest Cultural Resources Center Professional Papers, no. 23. Santa Fe: National Park Service, 1989.

Lord, Walter. *Day of Infamy.* New York: Henry Holt and Co., 1957.

Morison, Samuel Eliot. *The Rising Sun in the Pacific.* History of United States Naval Operations in World War II, vol. 3. Boston: Little, Brown and Co., 1948.

Pitt, Barrie, consultant ed. *The Military History of World War II.* New York: The Military Press, 1986.

Prange, Gordon W. *At Dawn We Slept.* McGraw-Hill, 1981. Reprint. New York: Viking Penguin, 1982.

Prange, Gordon W. *December 7, 1941.* New York: McGraw-Hill, 1988.

Reynolds, Clark G. *The Carrier War.* Alexandria, Virginia: Time-Life Books, 1982.

Spector, Ronald H. *Eagle Against the Sun.* New York: The Free Press, 1985.

Stephan, John J. *Hawaii Under the Rising Sun.* Honolulu: University of Hawaii Press, 1984.

Stillwell, Paul, ed. *Air Raid: Pearl Harbor!* Annapolis: Naval Institute Press, 1981.

Stone, Scott C. S. *Pearl Harbor: The Way It Was—December 7, 1941.* Aiea, Hawaii: Island Heritage, 1977.

Terzibaschitsch, Stefan. *Battleships of the U.S. Navy in World War II.* Translated and adapted by Heinz O. Vetters, and Richard Cox. London: Brassey's Publishers, 1977.

Theobald, Robert A. *The Final Secret of Pearl Harbor.* New York: Devin-Adair Co., 1954.

Wallin, Homer N. *Pearl Harbor: Why, How, Fleet Salvage and Final Appraisal.* Washington: U.S. Government Printing Office, Naval History Division, 1968.

Watts, Anthony J., and Brian G. Gordon. *The Imperial Japanese Navy.* Garden City, New York: Doubleday and Co., 1971.

Westwood, J. N. *Fighting Ships of World War II.* London: Sidgwick & Jackson, 1975.

Whitley, M. J. *Destroyers of World War Two.* Annapolis: Naval Institute Press, 1988.

Willmott, H. P. *Empires in the Balance.* Annapolis: Naval Institute Press, 1982.

Zich, Arthur. *The Rising Sun.* Alexandria, Virginia: Time-Life Books, 1977.

Picture Credits

Cover: National Archives.

Title page: National Archives

Japan 1854–1931: 12—National Archives.

Causes of War: 14—National Archives. 15—AP/Wide World.

The Plan: 18—(left and right) Naval Historical Center. 19—National Archives.

The Weapon: 23—(top) UPI/Bettmann, (bottom) National Archives.

Fuchida's Chart: 25—Franklin D. Roosevelt Library.

On the Way: 28—National Archives.

The Launch: 31—(top and bottom) National Archives.

Early Warnings: 32—National Archives.

Last Moment of Peace: 34—(top) U.S. Naval Institute, (bottom) National Archives.

Tora, Tora, Tora: 37—National Archives.

Torpedo Attack: 39—(top and bottom) National Archives. 40—(center and bottom) National Archives.

High-Level Bombing: 42—National Archives. 43—(top) Naval Historical Center, (bottom) National Archives.

Loss of Arizona: 44—(center) Naval Historical Center, (bottom) National Archives. 45—National Archives. 48–49—National Archives. 50—Prange Collection. 51—(top) National Archives, (bottom) Naval Historical Center.

Ford Island Naval Air Station: 53—(top and bottom) National Archives.

Hickam Field: 54—Smithsonian Institution. 55—U.S. Air Force.

Wheeler Field: 56—U.S. Air Force. 57—National Archives.

Kaneohe Naval Air Station: 59—(top) Prange Collection, (bottom) National Archives.

Ewa Marine Corps Air Station: 61—(top and bottom) courtesy, Colonel William Lucius, USMC ret.

Bellows Field: 63—U.S. Air Force.

They Arrived During the Fight: 65—(top and bottom) Smithsonian Institution.

Midget Submarine Attack: 66—(top and bottom) Naval Historical Center. 67—(top) Naval Historical Center, (bottom) National Archives.

Second Wave: 68—National Archives. 69—(top and bottom) National Archives.

Harbor Bombing: 71—(top and bottom) National Archives.

Sortie of the *Nevada*: 72—National Archives. 73—(top) National Archives, (bottom) Naval Historical Center.

Cassin and Downes: 75—National Archives.

USS *Shaw*: 76—National Archives. 77—(top and bottom) National Archives.

Hickam Field: 79—(top and bottom) National Archives, (center) U.S. Air Force.

Wheeler Field/Kaneohe Air Station: 80—(top and bottom) National Archives. 81—National Archives.

Ewa Air Station/Bellows Field: 82—courtesy, Colonel William Lucius, USMC ret. 83—Smithsonian Institution.

Final Action: 84—National Archives. 85—National Archives.

Honolulu Casualties: 86—National Archives. 87—(top and bottom) *Honolulu Star-Bulletin.*

Declaration of War: 88—National Archives. 89—National Archives.

Salvage: 92—(top) National Archives, (bottom) Naval Institute Press. 93—(top and bottom) National Archives. 94—(top and bottom) National Archives. 95—(top and bottom) National Archives. 96—(top and bottom) National Archives. 97—(top) National Archives, (bottom) Naval Institute Press. 98—(top) National Archives, (bottom) Naval Historical Center. 99—(top and bottom) National Archives.

Fate of the Commanders: 100—(top and bottom) National Archives. 101—(top and bottom) Naval Historical Center.

Fate of the Japanese Task Force: 102—courtesy, Colonel William Lucius, USMC ret.

Survivor's Tales: 104—National Archives. 107—National Archives. 109—National Archives. 111—National Archives. 112—courtesy, Richard Earl Laster.

Arizona Memorial: 114—National Archives. 115—Drawings by Jerry Livingston. National Park Service, Submerged Cultural Resources Unit.

Utah Memorial: 116—USS *Arizona* Memorial, National Park Service. 117—(top) USS *Arizona* Memorial, (bottom) Drawing by Jerry Livingston. National Park Service, Submerged Cultural Resources Unit.

Summary of Losses: 118—National Archives.

Chronology: 120—National Archives. 121—(top and bottom) National Archives.

Index

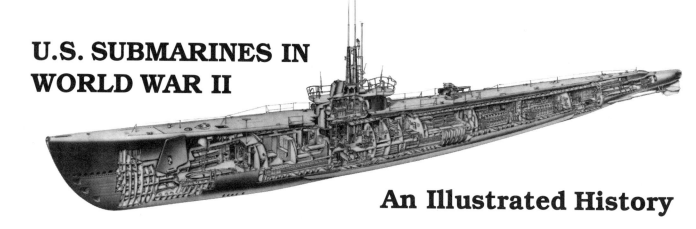